Victorian Villains

Prisoners from Newcastle Gaol 1871-1873

Best wishes

Barry Redfern

Barry Redfern

Tyne Bridge Publishing

in association with Tyne & Wear Archives

Acknowledgements

I would like to extend my sincere thanks to the following for their practical help and encouragement on this project. Henry Watson of Salford; Liz Rees, Chief Archivist, and all the staff of Tyne & Wear Archives Service; Anna Flowers and the team at Tyne Bridge Publishing; Newcastle Libraries & Information Service, particularly the staff at Local Studies; and to my daughter Linda Cain for proofreading the original and edited texts of the book.

Barry Redfern, Newcastle upon Tyne, 2006

The full unedited text is available to researchers at Newcastle Libraries & Information Service, Local Studies.

Photographs of the prisoners are copyright of Tyne & Wear Archives Service. The entire collection of forms and photographs is available to view at www.tomorrows-history.com. Search for 'Newcastle Gaol'.

Other illustrations are copyright of Newcastle Libraries & Information Service unless otherwise indicated.

Victorian Villains is published in association with Tyne & Wear Archives Service.

©Barry Redfern, 2006

ISBN 1 85795 108 5
978 185795 1080

Published by City of Newcastle upon Tyne
Newcastle Libraries & Information Service,
Tyne Bridge Publishing, 2006

www.tynebridgepublishing.co.uk

Printed by Elanders Hindson, North Tyneside

Contents

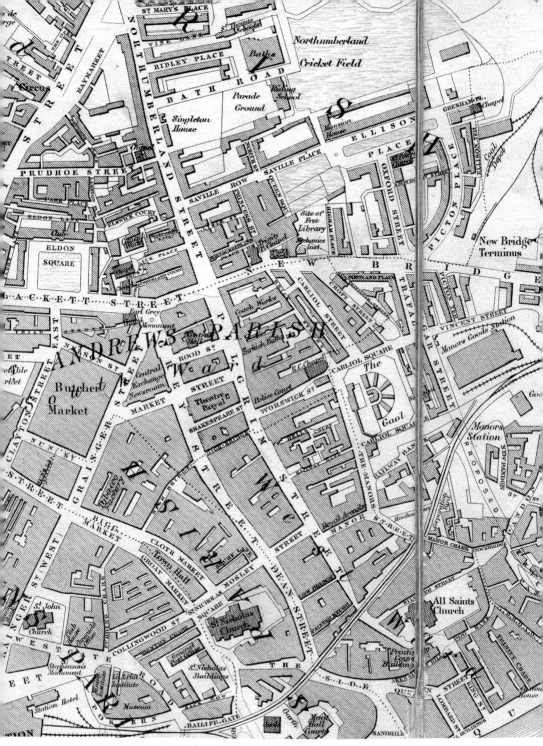

Central Newcastle from Reid's map of 1878.

Preface

Records of crime are common in UK archives, as it was in the interests of those primarily involved in record keeping to exercise control over anti-social activities. However, most records give only the bare facts – the crime, the name of the perpetrator and the punishment meted out. It is more difficult to picture the circumstances of the crime, the social and physical background against which it was committed, and even more so the face of the criminal.

We are extremely lucky to have a lone survivor of what must once have been a whole series of records that enable us to draw back the veil that has hidden the criminal environment of 19th century Newcastle. The volume of records and photographs of prisoners at Newcastle Gaol in the 1870s on which this book is based allows us to see the real people behind the often mundane crimes of poverty committed in the town (although there are some real villains too). Barry Redfern's painstaking research of court reports and local newspapers paints an evocative picture of everyday life in the teeming alleys and tenements. We see the newcomers from the countryside and from Ireland trying to make a new life in the city, the drunken soldiers and sailors, the women lured into prostitution, the children left to fend for themselves as well as the professional thieves and conmen and the injured dignity of the middle classes.

The stories that emerge are a mixture of social interaction, physical hardship, bad luck and stupidity. We read with amusement, compassion and incredulity of the harsh punishments handed down, and gain a unique insight into the lives our forebears lived in many of the same streets we walk down today – so different in many ways.

The preservation of this and many other records at Tyne & Wear Archives Service enables us to reach back and find out about life in the past in the most vivid way possible by seeing the faces and reading the actual words of those who have come before us. This book brings those records to a much wider public and we hope that you will enjoy it.

Liz Rees
Chief Archivist, Tyne & Wear Archives Service, 2006

G.　　R.

BY ORDER OF THE COMMISSIONERS OF H.M. PRISONS.

AT H.M. PRISON, CARLIOL SQUARE
(behind Pilgrim Street), NEWCASTLE-ON-TYNE.

Mr THOMAS S. Allison, F.A.I.

AUCTIONEER, VALUER and ESTATE AGENT,
Has received instructions to SELL BY PUBLIC
AUCTION, within the PRISON, on
MONDAY and TUESDAY, the 6th and 7th July,
1925,
commencing each day at 1.30 in the Afternoon,
THE WHOLE OF THE SURPLUS EQUIPMENT,
FURNITURE and FURNISHINGS,
comprising:—Office Furniture, Chest of Drawers,
Cupboards, Beds and Bedding, Blankets, Crockery,
Chairs (various), Cutlery, Bed-Boards, Stools,
Scales (various makes), Weighbridge (weighing
up to 8 tons), Tables, Laundry Utensils, Kitchen
Sundries, Coir Mats, Linoleum and other lots too
numerous to detail. See Catalogue.

On View, Friday and Saturday, the 3rd and 4th
July, from 9.30 a.m. to 4.30 p.m. each day.

Admission by Catalogue Only (price 6d each),
obtainable from the Controller, Prison Commis-
sion, Home Office, Whitehall, London, S.W.1; the
Officer in Charge, H.M. Prison, Carliol Square,
Newcastle-on-Tyne; or of the Auctioneer at his
Offices.

Auctioneer's Offices: 42, Borough Road, Sunderland. Auction Hall: 19, Tavistock Place, Sunderland. Tel., 1267. Telegraphic Address:
"Auctioneer, Sunderland." 4855

Newcastle Daily Journal and North Star advertises on 30th June, 1925.

A keepsake

The Prison Commissioners closed Newcastle Gaol in Carliol Square, Newcastle upon Tyne on 31st March 1925 and transferred the prisoners to Durham. (A short history of the prison appears at page 104). Furniture and fittings were auctioned in the prison on 6th and 7th July 1925 by Thomas S. Allison, Auctioneer of 42 Borough Road, Sunderland.

Arthur Thompson Watson was the man responsible for organising the auction. The Governor of the gaol, Major E.G. French, presented him with a keepsake salvaged from the prison to reward him for his work. It was a bound volume of prison forms with photographs; a register of certain categories of prisoners covering a period from December 1871 to December 1873.

The Watson family then lived in Hendon in Sunderland. Arthur Thompson Watson died in 1968 and the volume of forms and photographs passed to his son, Henry Watson. In 1998 Mr Watson, now living at Salford, Manchester, donated the bound papers to Tyne and Wear Archives at Newcastle upon Tyne. It was a generous and important contribution to Tyneside archives as very little in the way of artefacts and original documents have survived from the Newcastle Gaol.

The original binding of the collection was plain cloth covered boards with no lettering and was in a poor state. The spine was missing and the volume was covered with parcel tape. Experts at Tyne and Wear Archives Service dismantled the volume and took steps to conserve the individual pages. When this work was complete an exhibition of the forms and photographs was held at the Discovery Museum. The collection is held at Tyne and Wear Archives, Blandford Street, Newcastle upon Tyne under Access No. PR/NC/6/1. The material can be viewed there on microfilm. The entire set of forms and photographs can be seen on the Internet by visiting www.tomorrows-history.com and searching the collections for 'Newcastle Gaol'.

This book makes a selection of the photographs available in a printed format, describes the prison forms and their purpose and explores the background stories of the criminals and their crimes. It aims to show the value of the documents for genealogy and local history of social conditions and criminal justice.

No magistrates' court ledgers or police case files or papers have survived for this period. It has been possible to piece together some of the background stories from various sources including the Tyneside newspapers of the time. The local press did not report all cases appearing before the justices. On many occasions nothing would be reported, possibly because of lack of space in the newspapers or nothing of special interest in the proceedings.

A complete schedule of the prisoner names appears in Appendix No.1 with other categories of useful information. The research into this collection has revealed many groups or gangs of accomplices. These are listed in Appendix No. 2. It may be helpful to researchers and of interest to the general reader to know who they are. More detail about some of these gangs appears in the text and can be traced using the index.

Poor dwellings at the head of Long Stairs around 1880.

Prevention of Crime

P roceedings of the Newcastle upon Tyne Council November 9th, 1871 (page 15) PREVENTION OF CRIME. The following communication which had been received from the Home Office, was submitted to the Council.

Whitehall 28th October 1871

Sir: – I am desired by Mr Secretary Bruce to transmit to you the enclosed instructions and regulations in reference to the duties to be performed by Chief Officers of Police and Governors of Prisons under the Prevention of Crime Act (34 & 35 Victoria ch.112) which was passed in the last session of Parliament, and will come into operation on the 2nd of the ensuing month: and I am to request that you will move the Town Council of Newcastle-on-Tyne to take measures for causing the same to be carried into effect within their jurisdiction.

I am, Sir, your obedient servant H. S. P. Winterbotham

The letter and documents were referred to the Gaol and Watch Committee.

~

In the second half of the 19th century the authorities had to respond to a change in the manner of dealing with persistent criminals. Transportation to Australia had ended and provision had to be made for those prisoners who would have formerly been banished. National penitentiary prisons were developed for long serving prisoners. All prisons were brought under the control of the Prison Commissioners in 1877 and the closure of many small prisons in the provinces established a much more efficient system.

Alongside these changes came a strategy to prevent crime by introducing an extra penalty for persistent criminals. A man or woman with convictions for certain categories of offences would not only be sentenced for a new offence, but subject to proof of conviction for an earlier crime, would be liable to a further penalty as a recidivist. The legislation was known as the Prevention of Crimes Act; laws of that kind remained in force well into the 20th century.

The new act came into force on 2nd December 1871. Prison governors were required to prepare a formal record of prisoners convicted of certain offences specified in the act. The records were held and maintained by the Commissioner of the Metropolitan Police on behalf of the Secretary of State. The Governor of the Newcastle Gaol also kept copies for his own record. The collection donated to Tyne and Wear Archives by Mr Watson formed part of the Governor's records for the period December 1871 to December 1873.

Each record consists of a printed form for an individual prisoner with handwritten entries for the various categories set out on the document. There are a total of 225 forms in the collection but the net number of persons is 223. TWAS 1095 John Gordon and TWAS 1280 John Gordon the Younger are two convictions for the same person with different photographs. Similarly, TWAS 1084 Elizabeth Rule and TWAS 1223 Elizabeth Hill are the same person, but this time using the same photograph. Admissions to the Newcastle Gaol were averaging 2,000 per year at the beginning of the 1870s; therefore this collection of 225 forms represents a small proportion (5.6%) over two years.

A typical example of a prison form in this collection is that relating to Sabina Forbes alias Purvis or Clark or Elizabeth Cruddace (TWAS 1242), a 32-year-old married prostitute born in Newcastle upon Tyne.

The number (in this case 1242) at the top right corner of the form is the Tyne and Wear Archives (TWAS) number and does not form part of the original document. The date REPORTED TO THE SECRETARY OF STATE is usually recorded a few days after the offender has been released from prison. A prison form number appears below. Section 20 of the Prevention of Crimes Act 1871 specified stealing, breaking and entering, robbery and so forth, plus certain other offences such as uttering (presenting) forged documents and counterfeit notes and coin.

The next items are the personal details and description of the prisoner including distinguishing marks and a photograph. These were all very

REPORTED TO THE SECRETARY OF STATE, *June 14* 187 *3*

174

PARTICULARS of a Person convicted of a Crime specified in the 20th Section of the Prevention of Crimes Act, 1871.

Name and aliases } *Sabina Forbes Purvis, Clark, Elizabeth Cruddace*

PHOTOGRAPH OF PRISONER.

Description when liberated.

Age (on discharge)......... *32*

Height..................... *5.5*

Hair...................... *Brown*

Eyes...................... *Blue*

Complexion............... *Dark*

Where born............... *Newcastle on Tyne*

Married or single......... *Married*

Trade or occupation........ *Prostitute*

Any other distinguishing mark.................. } *Scar on upper lip, Blue mark on left arm*

Address at time of Apprehension......... *Newcastle on Tyne*

Whether summarily disposed of, or tried by jury .... } *Summarily*

Place and date of conviction............... *Newcastle on Tyne Jany 7/73*

Offence for which convicted .... *C S A money person*

Sentence .... *6 Cal Months HL*

If subject to supervision of police, when liberated, and for what period ..

If liberated on license, date when sentence will expire......................

Date when liberated .... *July 6/73*

Intended residence after liberation ...... *Newcastle on Tyne*

11

important to make a positive identification if the prisoner faced a further conviction. There is no information about the photographer the governor employed to take the portraits of the prisoners. Photography was in its infancy at that time but the profession was growing fast. In the Directory of Newcastle upon Tyne for 1873-1874 there are no less than 16 commercial photographers listed, rising to 20 in the following edition. There was probably a contract with one of those photographers to go to the prison when needed.

Next follows detail of the arrest and conviction. 'Summarily' means tried and sentenced by the magistrates sitting in the Police Court which was part of the police station at Manors. 'CJA money person' is an abbreviation meaning 'Convicted under the Criminal Justice Act of stealing money from the person.' Picking pockets or stealing purses would be typical examples. '6 Cal Month HL' means sentenced to be imprisoned for six calendar months and put to hard labour.

At the foot of the page there is the date of release from prison, 6th July 1873, eight days before Forbes' conviction and sentence were reported to the Secretary of State. Prisoners at that time served the exact sentence for summary convictions without remission. The 'Intended Residence' is never actually given, only the place, invariably Newcastle upon Tyne.

On the back of the form appear lists of 'Summary Convictions' before the magistrates and any convictions at the higher courts: the Quarter Sessions before a Recorder and jury; or the Assizes before a High Court Judge and a jury. Forbes had no higher court convictions but a run of nine summary convictions going back to 1864. Five were for stealing money from the person; clearly here was a prostitute habitually stealing from clients and others. The victim in the current conviction was a woman named Ellen Scott. A couple of assaults, a bye-law offence and an appearance for drunkenness complete the picture of someone leading an unruly life.

The form names the Newcastle Police officer, Police Constable 22 Amos Guntup, who could identify Forbes and prove the conviction. It is rare to see any information given about 'antecedents, associates &c.' although it is known from other sources that Forbes' accomplice was Margaret McCann, TWAS 1243, a hawker born at Newcastle upon Tyne, aged 22 years, with just two previous convictions. McCann was sentenced to two months imprisonment with hard labour.

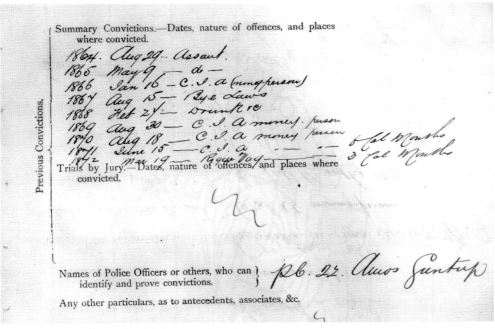

Summary Convictions.—Dates, nature of offences, and places where convicted.

1864. Aug 29 — Assault.
1865   May 9 — do —
1866   Jan 16 — C.I.A (young person)
1867   Aug 15 — Bye Laws
1868   Feb 2 — Drunk rc
1869   Aug 30 — C.I.A money. person
1870   Aug 18 — C.I.A money person   6 Cal Months
1871   June 15 — C.I.A —   3 Cal Months
1872   Mar 19 — Rogue Vag

Previous Convictions,

Trials by Jury.—Dates, nature of offences, and places where convicted.

Names of Police Officers or others, who can identify and prove convictions. } PC. 22 Amos Guntrip

Any other particulars, as to antecedents, associates, &c.

Detail from the back of Sabina Forbes' form.

Margaret McCann, 22, was Sabina Forbes' accomplice.

An example of a prisoner whose punishment was increased by the Prevention of Crimes Act is John Taylor TWAS 1285, a 26-year-old bricklayer.

He had several minor convictions. His conviction and sentence of one month hard labour on 16th June 1873 for stealing a trowel resulted in an additional sentence of one month hard labour to be served after the first.

The information written on the forms has, by and large, been verified by research. But prison officials did make mistakes. The photograph of TWAS 1275 Isabella Smith appears on the form of her accomplice

John Taylor, destined for two months' hard labour for stealing a trowel.

TWAS 1276 Mary Patterson, and vice versa. The conviction date on the form of TWAS 1177 Agnes Stewart should read 31st October 1872 not 1873. No photograph appears on the form of TWAS 1228 Ann Carr. The form for TWAS 1250 John Fox records him as convicted of shopbreaking. Fox actually pleaded guilty to, and was sentenced for, knowingly receiving goods stolen by shopbreaking.

Impudent Burglars

The first prisoner by conviction date in this collection took part in what the *Newcastle Daily Journal* described as an 'Impudent Burglary.' His name was Patrick O'Neill and his case illustrates how these archives link into the people, places and events already familiar to many local historians.

IMPUDENT BURGLARY IN HIGHAM PLACE

At the Newcastle Police Court yesterday, Patrick O'Neil (19), was charged before the Mayor, (R.B. Sanderson Esq.,) Ald. Sillick & Benjamin Plummer Esq., with having burglariously entered the house of Mr Joshua Bagnall, 6 Higham Place, and stolen therefrom two dozen silver plated forks and a like number of plated spoons together with several bottles of wine and spirits, during Thursday night and Friday morning.

Newcastle Daily Journal, Saturday August 26th, 1871

Higham Place, off New Bridge Street opposite the Lying In Hospital, is marked with an arrow. This a detail from a panorama of Newcastle around 1870 by James Storey. The houses are still there today beside the Laing Art Gallery.

The victim of the crime, Joshua Innes Bagnall, at the time of the 1871 census, lived with his daughters Mary (24), Eliza (15), sons William (22), Joshua (5) and two women servants. Bagnall, a publican, was the proprietor of the Oxford Music Hall in the Cloth Market. This establishment is famous as 'Balmbra's Music Hall' (after John Balmbra who owned the business ten years earlier at the time of the first performance of the Geordie anthem 'Blaydon Races.') The house on Higham Place was part of one of the earliest projects of Richard Grainger, the famous Newcastle builder and town developer, commissioned by Alderman William Batson, a prominent Newcastle Methodist.

On the night of the burglary, Miss Mary Ann Bagnall, one of Joshua Bagnall's daughters, arrived home at about quarter to midnight. She thought she heard a noise, but after looking around she satisfied herself that no one was in the house. At about three o'clock in the morning she was awakened by a loud ringing at the door. She and her sister went to open it and discovered three or four policemen standing outside. They informed her that the house had been broken into and asked her to make a search.

> She accordingly went and looked round and discovered that the drawers of the sideboard had been opened, and that several bottles of sherry, champagne, port and burgundy had been taken out. It was evident that the burglars had been indulging freely in wines and spirits for several bottles were lying on the table. In addition several pots of jam had been broken into and the room was in a dreadful state of confusion. She identified a bottle and two jam pots produced as being the property of her father.
>
> *Newcastle Daily Journal, Saturday August 26th, 1871*

Further evidence was given by PC Eaton who was on duty in Pilgrim Street at a quarter past two o'clock that morning. He saw O'Neill and several others coming up Bell's Court, talking loudly. Sensing something was wrong, Eaton made a grab for two of the men. O'Neill ran off and Eaton followed him, arresting him near the gaol. In the mean time the other men had got away. A bottle half full of sherry and two jam pots (identified by Miss Bagnall) were found in (O'Neill's) possession.

O'Neill was a 19-year-old native of Newcastle, described on his prison form as a 'shoe-black' with a scarred face and webbed feet. He already had two previous convictions. At 15 years of age he had been sent to prison for ten days, then to reformatory school for three years for stealing, then another seven days in gaol in February 1871 for a bye-law offence. He must have felt some irony when he was arrested near the town

The unfortunate Patrick O'Neill, 19, was a shoeblack.

gaol in Carliol Square as he was soon to spend a long time in that institution. O'Neill's accomplices, Francis McIntyre, a printer aged 19, and Robert O'Hara, a miller aged 18, and an 'old man named Thomas Finigan', were soon arrested and joined him in prison on remand. The report of the remand hearing for O'Neill's accomplices revealed more details about the crime.

THE BURGLARIES IN NEWCASTLE

At the Newcastle Police Court yesterday, two lads Francis McIntyre and Robert O'Hara, and an old man named Thomas Finigan, were charged, the two first named with having burglariously entered the house of Mr Joshua Bagnall 5 Higham Place

Newcastle Daily Journal, Tuesday August 29th 1871

Detective George Anderson gave evidence that he went to McIntyre's house on Friday afternoon and behind the clock face found a bottle which was half full of sherry and a quantity of raspberry jam. After a further search he found a large quantity cigars and pipes and on the next day found some more wine. All these items were identified by Miss Bagnall as her father's property. McIntyre acknowledged that it was part of the proceeds of the robbery from Mr Bagnall's.

Detective Anderson also visited the shop run by Finigan, a general dealer in Low Friar Street. He asked for Finigan who, according to his daughter, was lying drunk in bed. Anderson then asked the girl if she had bought any cutlery and she produced 14 forks and seven spoons, all later identified by Miss Bagnall. On Anderson's next visit to the shop, Finigan (now presumably sobered up) told him he paid five shillings to a young man he did not know for the forks and spoons. On Sunday morning Anderson traced O'Hara to a lodging house in the Side. O'Hara had six skeleton keys in his possession which he said he had got from McIntyre. He also admitted to selling the cutlery to Finigan for three shillings.

At the police station Finigan denied having seen any of the other prisoners before, but O'Hara made a statement that showed Finigan regularly fenced stolen property for him. The items included a gold watch and chain (sold for £1 and the proceeds of a robbery from the Belgrave Terrace house of the Rev. R.A. Thompson, Vicar of St Mary the Virgin, Rye Hill); a locket and a ring (sold for 3s 6d); and a silver butter knife, a pair of nutcrackers and a ladle, all part of the loot from the Bagnall burglary.

At the hearing the following Friday, O'Neill, O'Hara and McIntyre were committed for trial for the Higham Place burglary. O'Hara was also charged with the vicarage burglary and another. It emerged that O'Hara had gained entry there by lifting up a window of the bedroom where the vicar's daughter was sleeping. The magistrates decided to take no further action against Finigan; they had no moral doubt of his guilt but there was insufficient of evidence to secure his conviction.

According to the 1871 census, Thomas Finnigan [sic] had a shop and living accommodation at 10 Low Friar Street. He was a 60-year-old Irish general dealer living with his wife Margaret (61) and his grand-daughter Amelia (20), an upholsteress. The problem with prosecuting Finigan was the reliance on the evidence of his supposed accomplices, but the story reveals how easy it was for O'Hara to dispose of stolen goods.

The burglars appeared at the Newcastle Assizes starting on Monday 12th December 1871. O'Hara faced two additional charges of burglary. The judge 'Mr Baron Piggot' sentenced O'Neill to 18 months imprisonment (the longest prison sentence of the convicts in this collection), McIntyre to 12 months and O'Hara to five years penal servitude. O'Hara would be required to serve his sentence in one of the national penal institutions. McIntyre would have served his sentence at the Newcastle Gaol but does not appear in this collection.

The Side around 1880. Robert O'Hara was living in a lodging house here when he was arrested. It was still the main route into town for those who wished to avoid the tolls charged on the High Level Bridge.

The horse-whipping case

The notion of a man horsewhipping another as an act of revenge or to settle a grievance seems to belong in the realms of romantic fiction. But searching this collection revealed just such a case, which must have caused quite a scandal in Victorian Newcastle.

James Augustus Jobling was the son of Mark Lambert Jobling a prominent Newcastle solicitor and, for many years, Registrar of the District Probate Court at Westgate Road. Jobling Senior died in 1870, two years before the events that would bring the family name into disrepute. In November 1872, James Jobling was aged 26, single and described in some sources as a solicitor, but in other contemporary sources as a merchant or a grease manufacturer. His victim was Thomas Charles Grainger, the eldest son of Richard Grainger the architect, single and 45 years of age at the time of the attack upon him. It is not clear what profession he was following, but in the census of 1881 he was described as an 'annuitant' (living on an annuity).

James Augustus Jobling, a well-to-do young man. Prison must have come as quite a shock.

According to a report in the *Newcastle Courant* of Friday 29th November 1872, Jobling and Grainger had fallen out because Grainger had made derogatory comments about a young lady whom Jobling 'highly respected'. On the night of 16th November,

The Central Exchange around 1880. The building had been created by Richard Grainger.

Jobling sent a note to Grainger at the Central Exchange Art Gallery, asking him to meet a gentleman at Watkins Royal Exchange nearby. Grainger set off immediately. At the steps leading to the Royal Exchange, the short-sighted Grainger bent his head to see where he was going. At the same time Jobling, who was standing at the entrance, apparently waiting for Grainger, struck him a violent blow across the side of the face with the handle of a horsewhip. This blow resulted in a five-inch-long wound on Grainger's face. Two more blows, and two more wounds, followed. Because the attack was premeditated, the magistrates committed Jobling for trial at the Quarter Sessions and set bail of £200.

The identity of the lady, the nature of the defamatory remarks and where all that took place were not revealed in the press reports.

The Central Exchange and Reading Room mentioned above was created by Richard Grainger inside the triangle of buildings formed by Grey Street, Grainger Street and Market Street. The Exchange was destroyed by fire in 1901 and replaced by a handsome arcade of shops. Thomas Charles

Grainger was living nearby, when the 1871 census was taken, in a commercial hotel at 102 Grey Street.

Jobling appeared at the Newcastle Quarter Sessions on Sunday January 1st 1873 before the Recorder William Selby Seymour Esq.

At the trial, counsel for Jobling offered to plead guilty to common assault but that was rejected after lengthy legal argument, so Jobling pleaded guilty to wounding Thomas Charles Grainger. Jobling offered fulsome apologies to Grainger, both for the assault and the attack on his character. The Recorder had much to say before passing sentence. He appreciated that the punishment meted out to a man of Jobling's station in society would have a 'far more acute effect … than the same punishment would probably have upon a man in the lower ranks of life'. After Grainger had insulted the lady, rather than striking out in the heat of the moment, Jobling had spent three days planning his revenge, conduct the recorder considered neither fair nor honourable. However, because Jobling had made a full apology to Grainger, and because pleas for mercy had been made on his behalf, he would pass a relatively light sentence, of one month's imprisonment without hard labour. Jobling also had to provide sureties of £1,200 to keep the peace towards Grainger for two years.

The prison conditions Jobling had to endure are explored on page 104, but at least he was spared the hard labour. In the 1881 census Jobling lived at 23 Leazes Terrace, Newcastle, now 35 years of age, unmarried and looked after by one servant. At the same time, Grainger was living at 8 Ellison Place with two servants, he was also unmarried and recorded as 54 years of age although he was actually 58.

Masters must be protected

Scattered around this collection are 13 examples of men and women convicted of stealing from their employers. The magistrates usually took an unfavourable view of such offenders; the chapter heading is a quote from one of them. It is also interesting to note that the Tyneside newspapers tended to find space for these cases, whereas many other criminals in these records passed through the magistrates' court without appearing in the newspapers.

Walker and Emley was a firm of iron founders with premises in Westgate Road and Orchard Street, Newcastle. In 1873 they employed 'a respectable looking man', James Richley, aged 30 years, whose fall from grace for stealing trivets (supports for kettles etc.) was reported in the *Daily Journal* newspaper at the end of April that year.

'Respectable looking' James Richley

James Richley a respectable looking man was charged before Aldermen Dodds and Wilson at the Newcastle Police Court yesterday with having stolen metal trivets valued 3s 0d., the property of his employers Messrs Walker and Emley, ironmongers, Neville Street. The prosecutor did not press for heavy punishment as the prisoner had hitherto borne a good character, and had a wife and family to support. Alderman Dodds said it was a pity that the prisoner had placed himself in that position for such a trifling matter; but masters must be protected from dishonest servants, he was sentenced to seven days imprisonment.

Newcastle Daily Journal, Wednesday April 30th, 1873

River crimes

Stealing from employers often amounted to pilfering petty amounts of stock or money but the sheer weight of the following examples puts them into a different category.

John Bryan was a 29-year-old wherryman who moved material by boat on the Tyne for his employers Locke, Blackett & Co. of St Anthony's, Newcastle. The temptation put in his path when he was asked to transport lead was too much for John Bryan. He had the transport on the river, access to the metal and many contacts to dispose of it.

John Bryan the wherryman.

THEFT OF LEAD BY A WHERRYMAN.

Yesterday at the Newcastle Police Court, a wherryman, named John Bryan (29), was charged on suspicion before Alderman Graham and Mr B. Plummer with having stolen sundry pieces of lead the property of Messrs Locke, Blackett and Co., St. Anthony's. The prisoner was charged by the prosecutor to carry lead to and from various manufacturers on the river. Two pieces weighing 1¹/₂ cwts were missed from the works at St. Anthony's. Suspicion fell upon the prisoner who had been seen to carry some blocks, resembling the two pieces of lead missed from the riverside, on board his wherry. The prisoner pleaded guilty and the magistrates committed him to prison for four months.

Newcastle Daily Journal, Friday February 22nd, 1873

Mushroom Quay, near St Anthony's, 1886, where John Scott (see next page) was employed.

In a similar fashion John Scott, also 29 years of age and working beside the Tyne for Langdale & Co. at the Mushroom Quay fell into the same trap of temptation.

Both Scott and Bryan were mature married men, without previous convictions, who put their liberty, character and future employment prospects at risk for the sake of quick money. Scott somehow made off with more than two cwt of lead (about 122 kilograms) and that was to take him to gaol for an even longer period than Bryan.

John Scott looks much older than his 29 years.

THEFT OF LEAD

At the Newcastle Police Court yesterday, a man named John Scott pleaded guilty to stealing 2 cwt, 2 qtrs., 18 lbs., of lead from Messrs Langdale and Co.'s manure works, where he was employed, during the past two months, and was sentenced to six months hard labour.

Newcastle Daily Chronicle, Saturday November 30th, 1872

Embezzlement

Embezzlement is the term used to describe people stealing cash from their employers. It usually involves some sort of concealment of the crime with fraudulent entries in company records and so forth. Such tactics can often delay discovery by months or even years. Invariably the misconduct comes to light in time because greed leads to escalating thefts and eventually there is insufficient money to balance the books.

George Lee is a typical example. A 39-year-old family man with no history of committing crime, he worked as a travelling salesman for the well-

George Lee, who was tempted to embezzle his employer's money.

known Newcastle firm of stationers John Bowes and Co., Low Friar Street. Lee collected money from customers but in time it came to light that he was failing to record the payments and pay over the money to his employer. That failure cost him his liberty for three months and, as with others in this category, his character and prospects.

According to a report in the *Newcastle Courant* of Friday 11th April 1873, Lee had been working for John Bowes for five years. He had supplied goods worth £8 16s 8d to Mr Johnson, a grocer on Pilgrim Street. Mr Johnson paid his bill, but Lee did not record the payment in his book or pass the money on to his employer. After an investigation it was revealed that Lee had embezzled about £250 over the course of his employment. Lee pleaded guilty to the charge. He received 35 shillings a week salary plus travelling expenses and a commission of 2% on any increase in orders made upon the previous half year.

The defence counsel, Mr Forster claimed that for a man in the prisoner's position 35 shillings a week did not go a long way. He asked the Bench to remember that by giving the prisoner a heavy punishment, they would also punish his wife and his five children. Alderman Hedley said the bench had a duty to make an example which might deter others from following in the prisoner's footsteps, but as the prosecutor did not press for heavy punishment, they would pass a somewhat lenient sentence of three months' imprisonment.

Ezekiel Yates.

The case of Ezekiel Yates (or Yeates or Yetts) again involved a breach of trust.

Yates worked for Harvey and Davy & Co., tobacco dealers and snuff manufacturers, of Hanover Square, Newcastle. He was a married man, with no convictions, 35 years of age and born in Penrith.

Yates had worked for his employers for four or five years and had served

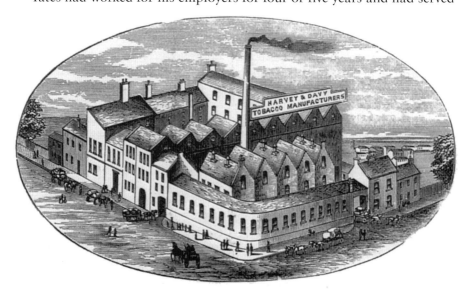

HANOVER TOBACCO FACTORY.

Hanover Square in the 1880s.

on the shop counter. The *Newcastle Daily Chronicle* for Saturday January 18th, 1873 records that he was charged with stealing tobacco and cigars as well as embezzling money despite receiving 'good wages and perquisites'.

Detective George Anderson found a box containing 109 cigars and a quantity of tobacco in the prisoner's house. Yates explained that the firm's employees were allowed so many cigars and so much tobacco every week. Anderson then decided to search Yates and found on his person 31 cigars and half a pound of tobacco.

The prosecuting counsel, Mr Hoyle, stated that if Yates pleaded guilty to theft, he was quite willing to withdraw the evidence relating to the embezzlement as the employers did not wish to be vindictive if Yates showed some contrition. The prisoner pleaded guilty and one of the magistrates, Mr Hammond, commented that if he had not, they would have had no choice but to indict him for trial at the Quarter Sessions. Yates was sentenced to six months' hard labour, a much lighter punishment than would have been imposed by the Quarter Sessions. Again, it was emphasised that breaking the trust of an employer was something that could not be overlooked.

Mary Patterson, left, and Isabella Smith.

The two petty thieves pictured above were accomplices. Because of a clerical error at the gaol the photograph of Isabella Smith, a 60-year-old widow born at Elsdon, Northumberland, was fixed to the prison form of her work colleague Mary Patterson, a 25-year-old married woman born at Newcastle upon Tyne, and vice versa. Neither woman had any previous convictions. In the 1871 census Isabella Smith, listed as a widow, 59 years of age, a char-woman, was living with her sons Thomas and George at Fleece Court, Newcastle. A short report in the *Newcastle Daily Journal* described how the women fell foul of the law by stealing poultry from their employer, John Brown, a poulterer of Blackett Street, Newcastle upon Tyne.

A domestic theft

In 1871 FitzHenry A. Kersey, a 62-year-old retired farmer from Suffolk, and his family lived at 4 Nixon Street, Newcastle. Sometime between November 1872 and April 1873 the family took into their employment and into their home a servant girl named Isabella Dodds. She was just 17 years old, born at Liverpool and unmarried. The Kersey family surely could not have known that Dodds had been released from prison at Newcastle on 2nd November 1872, after serving two months with hard labour for stealing money. Her stay in prison had not reformed her character.

According to local newspaper reports of April 1873, Dodds absconded from Nixon street, taking with her a gold watch, two gold chains, three gold seals, a gold ring and a quantity of clothing, all belonging to members of the Kersey household. She was arrested by Detective-officers George Anderson and Selby Fawcett, who found the watch and chains, as well as pawn tickets for the clothing, in her possession. She pleaded guilty at her trial and was sentenced to be imprisoned for four months.

Isabella Dodds.

Nixon Street was near Lovaine Crescent, pictured here in 1896. These pleasant terraced houses were off Sandyford Road on the site of Northumbria University.

Railway larceny

Dishonest employees were also found in the fast developing local and national railways. Railways were used to transport a wide variety of goods, as well as passengers. George Bell, a 24-year-old married man, working for the North Eastern Railway Company, had access to parcels. He could not resist interfering with them and that took him to the dock at the Newcastle Police Court.

George Bell.

THEFT OF GOLD WATCHES

At the Newcastle Police Court before Messrs H. Milvain and C.F. Hammond, a young man named George Bell was brought up on remand, charged with stealing two gold watches, valued at £36, or otherwise receiving them, well knowing them to have been stolen. Mr Bush appeared for the North Eastern Railway Company, the prosecutors in the case; and Mr J.E. Joel [Jonathan Edmondson Joel, Solicitor, 1 Newgate Street, Newcastle] defended the prisoner.

Newcastle Daily Chronicle, February 1st, 1873

On 12th October the two gold watches were sent in a parcel addressed to Mr Rosenburgh, watchmaker at 169, Westgate Road, Newcastle. The parcel arrived safely at Thirsk, after which it seemed to disappear without trace. However, a week before the court hearing, Detective Thorburn discovered that George Bell had been selling watches and arrested him. Bell claimed that he had found the parcel containing the watches at the Central Station. One was now in the possession of a watchmaker named Lyons, and the other had been stolen from his pocket.

Lyons, the watchmaker testified that Bell came to him in December and left a gold watch to be repaired. Bell said it was his own watch and that he

The Central Station in Neville Street was opened in August 1850 by Queen Victoria and Prince Albert and was rated one of the marvels of the railway age.

had found it near the theatre. The cost of the repair was £1 5s 0d, but he was never paid so he kept the watch.

David Garrit, a smith employed at Joicey's Works, Forth Banks said he bought a gold watch from Bell at the end of November for £2 payable in instalments. After two or three days Garrit returned the watch to Bell. Later he picked Bell's pocket and took the other watch 'for a lark'. He kept it for about a month and then sold it for £3. A young man named Lonsdale admitted that he bought the watch from Garrit just before Christmas and kept it until a policeman came to enquire about it, when he gave it up.

Defence counsel pointed out that Bell was unable to read and was deficient in intellect. The magistrates asked Dr Hume to examine Bell. He concluded that although Bell's intellect was not strong, he was morally responsible. The Bench then sent Bell to gaol for two months.

The final case in this chapter involves a prosecution by the railway police. According to a report in the *Newcastle Daily Journal* of Thursday 2nd January 1873, George Reay (30) a railway guard, Robert Hardy (21) a signalman, and Thomas Pearson (31) a pilot guard, were charged with stealing one and a half gallons of beer, the property of their employers, the North Eastern Railway Company.

George Reay.

On Saturday morning, 15th December a truck containing barrels of beer came attached to a train from Berwick. It was left near the Trafalgar Goods Station (this marshalling yard was close to the Newcastle Gaol, in Carliol Square). Mr Davison, one of the foremen at the Trafalgar Goods Station was passing at seven o'clock in the morning, when he noticed Reay, Hardy and Pearson and another man named Johnson (who was not in custody) standing around the beer truck. The next time Davison passed that way, 20 minutes later, he saw the prisoners still standing about the wagon, and Johnson coming from underneath it. Mr Davison examined the truck and found one of the beer casks placed on its end and a quantity of beer taken out. All the prisoners were close together. Davison reported the incident; the men were arrested and found guilty. Each was sentenced to four calendar months imprisonment with hard labour.

Robert Hardy.

George Reay was a married man born in Scotland and Thomas Pearson was single and born at Humshaugh. Robert Hardy also single

Thomas Pearson.

The Trafalgar Goods Station, centre, and Carliol Square Gaol, far left, in this detail from James Storey's panoramic view of Newcastle in the 1870s.

was born at Corbridge. In the 1871 census Robert Hardy was living in the lodging house of Ann Brown at 4 Regent Street, Newcastle upon Tyne. His occupation was recorded as engine cleaner.

What criteria the magistrates used for the level of punishment from one case to another are not known. However, in this last case, these three offenders, of previous good character, stole the equivalent of four pints of beer each. Their punishment equalled one month's hard labour for each pint of beer.

The state of the Newcastle police

In December 1871 when the Prevention of Crime Act came into force there were many questions being asked about the state of the local police force at Newcastle upon Tyne.

Police forces, as we know them today, were formed in the 1830s in London and the boroughs, but a little later in the shire counties. Before that an unpaid and untrained local citizen took on the job of parish constable and worked with the magistrate to deal with criminals detained, for the most part, by the general public. Investigation was largely a matter of the people banding together when needed to gather information and seize offenders, take them to a constable, then to a magistrate and thence to gaol. Parliament passed legislation to stop the appointment of parish constables in April 1873.

The authorities at Newcastle had one abortive attempt at forming a police force. That initiative lasted from November 1832 to September 1833; the public did not take to it. Later legislation gave the boroughs no option but to have a police force, so by the 2nd May 1836 the Newcastle Borough Police was in permanent action on the streets of Newcastle. The officer in charge was Superintendent John Stephens.

There were many developments over the next 35 years. The headquarters of the new force was established at Manors in a new building designed by John Dobson, with purpose-built cells for holding prisoners. The prison inspectorate reported favourably on the condition of the cells over this period. There is something odd about the 1871 Census Return for Manors Police Station; it records 22 prisoners in the building but no staff! Perhaps it had something to do with the shifts worked by the police officers.

The building included the Manors Police Court mentioned regularly in press reports on people in this collection. It replaced the Guildhall as a venue for summary hearings and examinations by the magistrates. This move brought the police and the magistrates close to the location of the town gaol in Carliol Square. Quarter Sessions and Assizes for Newcastle upon Tyne continued to be held at the Guildhall.

A former hospital on Westgate Road (formerly called Westgate Street) at

The first police station and the Manors Police Court was conveniently near Carliol Square Gaol, near the rear of John Dobson's Royal Arcade, on Manor Chare, and adjacent to Holy Jesus Hospital at the centre of this picture. The gaol is right of centre. A detail from James Storey's panorama of Newcastle in the 1870s.

Thornton Street was taken into use as a police station.

By 1871 a police barracks with upwards of 30 unmarried police officers were living there in what were known as No. 1 and No. 2 Mess. Around the station were houses or flats for married policemen and their families. There

The Westgate police station in 1915.

was another police station at Laurel Street, Elswick that had seven unmarried constables living there. Another at the Ouseburn had 13 unmarried officers in the barracks and a resident Superintendent, Thomas Watson and his family. Another Superintendent, James Wallace, and his family were resident at Prudhoe Street Police Station in the centre of the town, also with a police barracks but only one constable was there when the census was taken.

Over the 35 years or so to 1871-3, the authorities had steadily built up a network of police stations around the town and provided accommodation for a large part of the force. The command structure comprised a chief constable and five superintendents who were based at Manors, Thomas Scott; Prudhoe Street, James Wallace; Ouseburn, Thomas Watson; and Laurel Street, John Bell. There was also a head of detectives, Detective Superintendent Edward Moore. All these stations were connected by telegraph in 1868, and steps were taken later to connect up to the Mansion

Policemen outside the Westgate police station in 1870.

House and with the Northumberland authorities and police via the Moot Hall.

The overall establishment of the force in 1871 was said to be 173, including 130 constables of various classes, but the actual strength was short by 21 constables. The two or three years leading up to the implementation of the Prevention of Crimes Act proved to be a demanding and testing time for everyone having anything to do with the Newcastle Borough Police.

In 1868 the Watch Committee appointed Captain W.C. Sylvester as Chief Constable. He had been Chief Constable of Salford up to that time. By April of 1869, notes were appearing in the Watch Committee Minutes about Captain Sylvester having great problems with his personal affairs and being under threat of bankruptcy. In July the same year Sylvester, unable to resolve his problems, offered his resignation which was accepted. The new Chief Constable was Captain Samuel James Nichols, 30 years of age born at Shrewton, Wiltshire and appointed at a salary of £400 per annum plus certain expenses. He was sworn in to his new office at the Manors Police Court on 27th September 1869. He settled with his family at 23 St Mary's

Terrace. At the 1871 census the household comprised Captain Nichols, his wife, two daughters, two sons and two servants.

Captain Nichols had an abrasive management and discipline style that the men under his command could not accept. There were only about 130 constables on the establishment of the Newcastle Borough Police when full. During 1870 and 1871 the constables began leaving in droves to seek other work. A Newcastle Council meeting heard that about 100 men had resigned over that year or so. New recruits were found but the force remained some 21 men (about 15%) short of the establishment. To be fair to Captain Nichols, some of the dissatisfaction was about pay; the police pay rates at Newcastle were below comparable boroughs elsewhere. The policing experience of many years was draining out of the Newcastle Borough Police and it was becoming staffed largely by raw recruits drawn from rural districts and unused to urban life. In August of 1871 one of the local newspapers indulged in some wry comment on this situation.

A general theme of conversation in the town at present is the number of new and unfamiliar faces to be seen in the borough police. Has there been a general strike in the force, and have the authorities, like the master engineers, been importing new men from Woolwich? That idea is indeed at once refuted by the physique and accent of the men which at once proclaim their descent from the Land o'cakes*. Very recently caught, most of them seem to be indeed; and I should suppose the thieving fraternity must be having a jolly time of it, missing the vigilant and instructed eye of our old and tried constables, who have all disappeared so suddenly and mysteriously. It is said to be very amusing to watch the demeanour of some of these hulking fellows, who are evidently more at home in a ploughed field than in their present situations, when called to give evidence at the Police Court. They get but badly through their story as a rule; and yet there is some consolation in observing that they have not yet got to heart the words 'Habit and repute, your worship.'

Newcastle Daily Journal, Friday August 25th, 1871

(*'Land o'cakes' means Scotland – from a poem by Robert Burns.)

The last remark must have referred to piece of police jargon of the day for describing suspects, reputed thieves, rogues and vagabonds.

The mention of the 'master engineers' is a reference to the fact that in 1871 there had been a huge strike of engineering tradesmen in the great factories on Tyneside, such as Hawthorn Leslie, Armstrong's and the like. The directors of these factories drafted in workers from elsewhere in England and Scotland and the continent. There was severe disorder at the factories and on the streets, reaching riot proportions at times. The policing demands were too heavy for the Newcastle force alone and reinforcements were brought in from the Durham and Northumberland Constabularies to assist and support the local police. That strike lasted for many months and ended in October 1871. It was a time of great pressure on the Newcastle force of inexperienced constables.

There was another deep problem in the force during 1871, and that was smallpox. At a meeting of the Watch Committee, on 4th April, the Police Surgeon, Dr William Rayne, reported two cases of smallpox in the force. The first was an officer in his family home at Bulmer Street, and the second was an officer in the police barracks at Prudhoe Street. The surgeon recommended that the Prudhoe Street Barracks should be closed. He also recommended that every member of the police force should be vaccinated by the 'Public Vaccinator who had possession of Vaccine Lymph in sufficient quantity.' That was a very sensible course of action for public servants likely to be exposed to infection in their duties. However, at the Watch Committee the following week 'The Chief Constable reported that no member of the Force had availed themselves of the recommendation of the committee on the subject of vaccination.' No names are quoted for the victims. There were several police officers living in Bulmer Street at the time of the 1871 census, William Newton, Joseph Dixon and George Martin, so the infected officer could have been any one of them.

By the 28th April, other cases had occurred at Prudhoe Street and the Watch Committee ordered the station closed and that all subsequent cases of smallpox should be sent there. Up to ten officers were ill with smallpox at that time. On 9th June, the Chief Constable reported to the committee 13 cases of smallpox in the force and one death. These figures are close to 10% of the actual strength of the force at the time. Nothing more was recorded until 22nd December, when the Watch Committee were informed of four

cases of smallpox in the force which had been traced back to the Police
Cottages at Spital Tongues 'about three weeks ago'. As the cottages were
unfit for habitation, the Watch Committee resolved that 'the officers of the
force be sent to the Small Pox Hospital'.

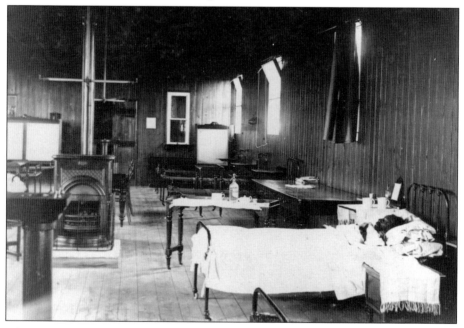

The smallpox isolation hospital on the Town Moor, 1898.

All of these pressures of work, pay, discipline, sickness and low morale
came to a head when a majority of members of the Newcastle Borough
Police presented a memorial to the Town Council on 6th September 1871.
The memorial was signed on behalf of 101 members of the force, that is to
say, about 66% of the existing strength. They complained about the activities of the Chief Constable Captain Nichols, 'the partial way he dealt with
them', 'the treatment to which they are subject from him,' and 'great injus-
tices in the disposal of appointments to the superior ranks'. The Town
Council were asked to remove their several grievances 'and so to prevent the
necessity of their resigning their situations and seeking other employment'.
There was also a request to 'institute such an inquiry into the merits of the
case as may seem requisite, and grant them such redress as to your worship-
ful body seem meet'. The members of the council, after some discussion,
referred the memorial to the Watch Committee.

A couple of days later, on 8th September, an editorial appeared in the *Daily Journal* identifying this action, to all intents and purposes, as a police strike: 'The police, however, have themselves as good as struck, their grievance, it appears, being partly one of wages and partly their treatment at the hands of the Chief Constable. This is an unpleasant state of affairs, and deserves to be thoroughly and fully enquired into. In so far as the wages of policemen who are below the rank of other workmen, it is evident that the disproportion must cease else we shall never have an efficient staff of police. The conduct of the Chief Constable is another matter and should be impartially investigated.'

The words 'strike' or 'police strike' were freely used from that time in connection with this affair. The Watch Committee received the memorial and, early in October, held a hearing of upwards of 20 members of the force explaining their complaints and describing their experiences. The Chief Constable responded to all of these matters. On 6th October 1871 the members of the Watch Committee gave their decision: 'None of the cases thus investigated appeared to be of a character to justify further interference. They are sensible of the importance of preserving good feeling between the Chief Constable and the Police Force, an object that the committee have always endeavoured to promote and they have given such directions as appeared to them to be necessary with reference to this object and which they accept will be effectual. Resolved accordingly'.

The *Daily Journal* summed up the police complaints at the hearing in this way: 'The conduct of the present Chief Constable is such that that your memorialists cannot act with comfort to themselves or justice to the public; that they consider themselves unjustly treated by the Chief Constable in trivial matters, that the powers entrusted to him are exercised in a very harsh manner and offences of the most trivial nature meet with very unfair

The unpopular Captain Nichols depicted in a local newspaper.

43

and tyrannical treatment at his hands; and that any attempt being made by your memorialists for hearing of their respective complaints, the Chief Constable declines to hear them, and on several occasions used threatening and unbecoming language to your memorialists.' (*Newcastle Daily Journal* Saturday 7th October, 1871.)

The last couple of points here are significant and reveal an important failing in the presentation of their complaints. Hindsight is a wonderful thing, yet it is clear these men should have planned and prepared more carefully, and appointed a persuasive spokesman, legally qualified if possible. A failure by the Chief Constable at least to hear matters of grievance was clearly wrong, and if that had been properly proved and supported by witnesses to the foul language as alleged, then perhaps they may have made some progress. As it was, the Watch Committee, the Town Council and reports in the local press treated the complaints as trivial and not worth pursuing. However, the authorities might have saved themselves a lot of future grief if they had seen the underlying message written on the wall and treated the issue more seriously.

The 'memorialists' held two meetings to discuss their options. Under a newspaper headline STRIKE OF THE NEWCASTLE POLICE FORCE, comments by the chairman at the meetings were reported 'Great numbers of the men in the force were appointed to the ranks; and many of the old constables before him knew perfectly well that within the past eighteen months or two years, many of the old and efficient policemen had quitted the force, and that there had been a large importation of new men. So naturally the force was in an inefficient state – owing to their Chief Constable and the treatment they had received from him.'

Part of an editorial in the same newspaper said: 'It is obvious however, they (the men's complaints) point rather to certain overstrainings of wholesome discipline than anything on the part of the Chief Constable savouring of deliberate tyranny or gross incapacity. The regulations alluded to cannot, at any rate, be the regulations of Captain Nichols himself. They must have been framed by the Watch Committee and all the Chief Constable can have done must have been to carry them out, in the opinion of the men, with undue vigour. If the force then has become so utterly demoralised, as the men themselves represent it to be, must we not be led to the conclusion that they are, in part at least, responsible for their own demoralisation.'

The editorial writer was correct in assuming that the Watch Committee had framed the regulations for the force. This had been done on 5th March 1869 six months before the arrival of Captain Nichols. The regulations were in a booklet called The Borough Police Constables' Guide issued by the Watch Committee.

Section Three of the Guide laid down clear and minute instructions for the duties of every officer from the Chief Constable to an ordinary constable. There were many ways in which a constable might find himself in breach of these orders and the Chief Constable was empowered

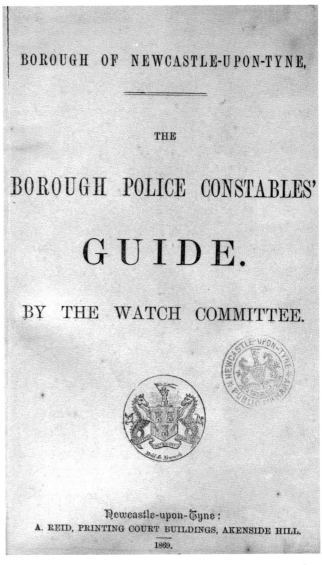

BOROUGH OF NEWCASTLE-UPON-TYNE,

THE

BOROUGH POLICE CONSTABLES' GUIDE.

BY THE WATCH COMMITTEE.

Newcastle-upon-Tyne:
A. REID, PRINTING COURT BUILDINGS, AKENSIDE HILL.
1869.

to admonish or reprimand for such shortcomings or refer officers to the Watch Committee. The Chief Constable also had the power to suspend officers and the petitioners asked for that power to be transferred to the Watch Committee. There were provisions under the Municipal Corporations Act 1835 for police officers to be fined at the magistrates' court for neglect of duty or disobedience of lawful orders. These powers were used from time to time, as in the case of Constable William Greenhow for example. According to a report in the *Newcastle Daily Chronicle* of Saturday April 26th, 1873, a police superintendent had telegraphed Laurel Street police station to tell Greenhow to attend the police court to give evidence in a case of obstruction. Greenhow was in his bedroom brushing his trousers at the time and refused to go! He was found guilty of disobeying orders and fined £2 plus costs.

Zealous enforcement of these powers and regulations may well have been the root cause of problems in the force. Eighty-five officers of the Newcastle Borough Police submitted their resignations, equal to about half the establishment, or more if account is taken of the shortfall of 21 officers. If the figures in these sources are reliable then the Newcastle Borough Police lost 185 officers in a period of two years or less. Why? Something was wrong and surely it could not all have been about rates of pay. The authorities had backed the Chief Constable and, despite one or two offers from prominent Newcastle citizens to mediate in this affair, no further steps were taken to investigate complaints against him. The Watch Committee moved to deal with the emergency and invited men of the town to be sworn in as special constables, but there seems to have been no great rush to take up the opportunity. Under the local act governing the Newcastle police (Newcastle upon Tyne Improvement Act 1865, Section 85) the officers could not resign without notice unless given written permission by the chairman of the Watch Committee. There is no record of such permission being given, so these men would have to work one month's notice, allowing the Watch Committee some time to find replacements. Urgent steps were taken to bring in new recruits, back-up assistance was provided by the Durham and Northumberland Constabularies, extra duty pay was authorised for the officers remaining in the force and one of the first actions of the Watch Committee was to increase the pay of the police.

That was the state of the Newcastle Borough Police Force coming up to December 1871 and the prosecution of the first convicts forming this prison form collection. About the only positive factor was increased pay, but in other respects they were below strength, staffed largely by new recruits, vastly inexperienced and morale must have quite a problem. Yet there was sufficient activity by this inexperienced force to fill the Newcastle Gaol well towards capacity in the period 1871 to 1873.

The names of the Newcastle Police Officers and the North Eastern

A mounted policeman at Westgate police station around 1870.

Railway Police involved with the convicts in this collection appear in the schedule at Appendix 1. Railway police forces had existed since 1830 in parts of the country. The North Eastern Railway Police was formed in 1854 following the amalgamation of several railway companies. There are around 130 different police officers listed on the prison forms and many are credited with several cases each.

Some police officers seem to have been particularly active thief-takers. The name of Detective Officer George Anderson appears no less than 14 times. He was the officer who investigated the 'Impudent Burglary' described in the opening chapter. Anderson was born at Tanfield, Co. Durham c1831 and at the 1871 census was living in one of the houses or apartments attached to the Westgate Police Station with his wife Dorothy (from Benwell) three daughters and one son Ralph, then four years old. By 1881 the Andersons had moved to 7 Lord Street, the first three daughters had left home and there was now another daughter in the family Margaret (nine) and a son William (six). George Anderson had not risen in the ranks, but his cases recorded in this collection suggest he was a thorough and conscientious detective. His age and the fact that he was still in the force between 1871-1873 shows that he was not part of the mass resignations described above. Amongst his cases were the two young housebreakers, Henry Leonard Stephenson and Michael Clement Fisher, described on page 88. His work seems to have been mainly on the western side of the town. It is also apparent he had good general knowledge of the families on his 'patch.' The girls in the following story are not part of the collection.

ROBBERY BY LITTLE GIRLS IN NEWCASTLE

At the Newcastle Police Court yesterday (Thursday) before Aldermen Hedley and Pollard, Ann Hodgson and Mary Ann Butler aged respectively fourteen and thirteen years, were charged with breaking into an unoccupied house on 29th November and stealing a large number of bottles, the property of James Hillyard. In defence the prisoners said that they had been asked into the house, to warm themselves, by some girls, and the latter had also asked them to go upstairs to get some coals, and in the meantime the girls went away, leaving them in the house. Detective George Anderson said he knew Hodgson's father to be a drunken lazy man, who would not work. He had cautioned him on several occasions for the manner in which he was neglecting his children and allowing them to roam the streets as they liked. The magistrates sent each of the prisoners to gaol for ten days and intimated that in the meantime steps would be taken to send them to a reformatory school.

Newcastle Courant, Friday December 1st, 1871

Another detective mentioned 17 times in this collection is Detective Officer Alexander Martin. He appears to have worked in the centre of the town. The curious thing about Martin is that his career seems to have survived being prosecuted for assault on a suspect. It is surprising he was not dismissed or required to resign.

Despite his punishment, Martin continued to pursue his duties with zeal. Just the following night, Martin and Detective Officer Selby Fawcett caught two men (James Loxley and Robert Cruddace robbing another in an entry off the Side, see page 120). It was also Martin who arrested Agnes Stewart and Richard Bradshaw for robbing a German man in the street.

Martin's colleague, Detective Officer Selby Youter Fawcett also lived in the police accommodation at Westgate, next door to George Anderson. Fawcett was 43 in 1871, born at Heddon-on-the-Wall, Northumberland, and living with his wife Margaret and three sons, including twin boys. The elder son Edward (14) was a telegraph boy; the Victorians were on the threshold of a communications revolution and the telegraph was proving to be very popular for business, public services and private use. Fawcett was also a very active member of the 'Detective Force', as it was known in those early days, with 16 convicts in the collection listed to him.

Lastly, from amongst the uniform constables, PC 20 Joseph Relfe stands out as active in arresting criminals. He dealt with the case of William Smith, got assaulted for his trouble, but showed he could handle a rough customer when required.

William Smith, see following page, a 25-year-old printer and a native of Sheffield, was sentenced to two months hard labour. He had no previous convictions. Constable Joseph Relfe prospered by his industry and by the time of the 1881 census he was a sergeant and living with his wife and two sons at 73 Sycamore Street. Ten years later he had left the police and was the caretaker of the Liberal Club at 22 Park Road.

SUSPECTED ROBBERY IN NEWCASTLE

At an early hour yesterday morning, PC Relfe, whilst on duty at the Stockbridge, Newcastle, came in contact with a man named William Smith, who was carrying a small brass pair of office scales, some weights and steel pens. On the officer accosting him Smith commenced a violent attack with the scales upon him, and the officer was required to freely use his staff before he could secure his prisoner. After great difficulty he was got to the police station where his wounds which he received in the course of the conflict were dressed by the doctor. He was afterwards locked up on suspicion of having broken into some premises.

William Smith

Newcastle Daily Chronicle, Monday February 10th, 1873

Captain Nichols was Chief Constable throughout the period of this collection and survived in the post until the end of 1898. His career at Newcastle was dogged by complaints about his management style and there were several more enquiries. Many officers continued to leave the force during his tenure. In 1898 290 police officers out of a force of 298 signed a petition complaining to the council. A real fear arose amongst the authorities and the residents that government inspectors would not certify the force as efficient because of Captain Nichols. The government grant for the force would then be lost.

A thorough enquiry by the council found in favour of the men. An independent enquiry into allegations that Captain Nichols had 'manipulated and squandered' money in recreation funds cleared the Chief Constable of any misconduct. However, a petition from the general public to the town council asked for the resignation of Captain Nichols. The petition was considered by the Watch Committee and accepted. Captain Nichols tendered his resignation the same day, 2nd December 1898. He left with a pension of £400 a year. In February 1899 friends and admirers presented him with an inscribed silver salver and 1,000 guineas.

Silver Street, which leads down to Stockbridge, photographed in 1884. It was a short distance to the police station at Manors when PC Relfe arrested William Smith.

A very bad character

It was not an offence in Victorian times for a woman to accept payment for a sexual relationship, nor is it today. The real legal and social problem involves the public nuisance of soliciting and the deeper impact of underworld control of prostitution, living on immoral earnings, managing brothels, the spread of disease and the encouragement of the degradation of women.

Twenty of the women appearing in this collection are described as prostitutes on their prison forms. But here is one those anomalies of statistics – not one of them was actually imprisoned for prostitution as such. All of them were gaoled for theft. Mary Ann Ross aged 34 years (according to her prison form), reported in the press as 'A very bad character', provides a typical example of how prostitutes lured men, often drunk, into vulnerable situations then robbed them. There are other women in the collection who were not described as prostitutes but clearly were active in that way. Some of their stories appear elsewhere in this book.

Mary Ann Ross.

At the Newcastle Police Court yesterday Mary Ann Ross, 35 years of age, a very bad character, this being her 31st appearance, was sentenced to six months hard labour for stealing 4s 10d from a man named Bernard Duffy in a house in Church Walk, about one o'clock on Tuesday.

Newcastle Daily Chronicle, Saturday October 26th, 1872

Mary Ann Ross actually had an amazing list of 32 previous convictions, all followed by imprisonment. The first was six months' hard labour on 12th June 1865 for stealing money from the person. For the last offence she had served 14 days in the Newcastle Gaol from 19th September 1872 for drunkenness, so had only been out of prison a matter of three weeks before her court appearance on 25th October 1872.

Ross was the eldest of those listed as prostitutes alongside a woman named Phillis Robinson, also recorded as 34 years of age although a local newspaper reported her as 32. Here again was the same scenario as Ross but more detail is known.

ROBBERY IN NEWCASTLE

At the Manor's Police Court yesterday before Mr H. Milvain and Mr C.F. Howard, Phillis Robinson, 32 years of age, was charged with stealing £14 from William Lockwood Hunter, in a house in Thornton Street on Tuesday evening. It appeared from the evidence of the prosecutor at about five o'clock on Tuesday afternoon he was going along Clayton Street, when two females, the prisoner being one of them, came and asked if he would stand a glass of ale. He consented and, in addition to treating them to

Phillis Robinson.

some ale, he gave each of them a pie, because they said they were very hungry. After leaving them he went towards the Cattle Market and the prisoner who had followed him along, came up to him again and asked if he would stand another three half-pence, and ultimately induced him to go to a house in Thornton Street, where she robbed him. Shortly afterwards, however, with the assistance of a woman who lives as a servant in the house, he got £13 from the prisoner. Sentenced to one month hard labour.

Newcastle Daily Chronicle, Friday April 25th, 1873

Robinson had six previous court appearances and prison sentences noted on her prison form. The list includes many convictions for vagrancy and prostitution, drunkenness, assaulting a constable and nine court appearances for theft leading to prison sentences ranging from two to six months.

The youngest of the twenty prostitutes was Catherine Kelly, a girl of 17 who had been born in Nottingham. Her offence had nothing to do with prostitution. She was sentenced to three months imprisonment for stealing clothing from a bothy (a small building) which was the gardener's residence in the grounds of Elswick Hall. This mansion in the suburbs of Newcastle upon Tyne was then occupied by Christian Allhusen, chairman of the Newcastle Chemical Company based at Newcastle Quayside. Her accomplices were Alice Mulholland an 18-year-old hawker and Jane Carlisle, alias Shaw, a 29-year-old

Catherine Kelly.

Alice Mulholland, left, and Jane Carlisle.

Elswick Hall around 1910, after its grounds had become a public park.

HOUSEBREAKING IN NEWCASTLE

At the Newcastle Police Court yesterday before the Mayor (Mr R. Cail) and Mr Ald. Dodds, Jane Carlisle alias Shaw, 29, Margaret McIntyre alias Neighton, 28, Catherine Kelly, 17, and Alice Mulholland 18 years of age, were charged with breaking into a bothy situated in the grounds of Mr C. Allhusen, Elswick Hall, on Wednesday afternoon and stealing five cotton bedsheets, three linen pillow cases, a pair of boots, a coat and a handkerchief. About half past four o'clock on Wednesday afternoon, Detective Officer Selby Fawcett observed the prisoners in Rye Hill and was proceeding towards them, when they ran away. He followed them and ultimately, with the assistance of some civilians, took them into custody, and found the articles mentioned in their possession, but did not know of the robbery at that time. Suspecting that they had stolen the things he took them to the Westgate Police Station. In the evening a report of the bothy having been broken into was given to the police and afterwards the property was identified. The prisoners pleaded guilty and were sent to jail. Neighton for six months, Carlisle for two months and the other two prisoners for three months each.

Newcastle Daily Chronicle, Friday April 18th, 1873

hawker.

Also involved was a woman named Margaret McIntyre, alias Neighton, who does not appear in this collection, but may have been the ringleader as she served six months imprisonment.

Kelly already had two previous convictions in her short life, seven days for drunkenness in 1872 and another seven days in prison for a bye-laws offence in February 1873 (probably connected to her activities as a prostitute).

The newspaper reports of the case of Mary Erskine Christie in September 1872 provide an example of a prostitute working with male accomplices (probably one them was her husband) to rob an elderly man in the street. The tactics here were for the men to hang around and leave it to Christie to importune the old man, a boilersmith from Blackhill, who must surely have been under the influence of drink to allow the prostitute to steal his watch and other things, then allow himself to be led across the High Level Bridge and be abandoned there. It would appear that the male accomplices could not be linked to the act of theft, so Thomas Christie and Michael Moran were charged with loitering for an unlawful purpose. The

SUSPICIOUS CHARACTERS

Yesterday morning at the Newcastle Police Court Thomas Christie, 36, and Michael Moran, 25, were charged with being on the streets for an unlawful purpose and were sent to prison. Christie for three months and Moran for one month. Mary Erskine Christie alias Campbell was also charged with frequenting Queens Lane for the purpose of committing a felony. A small boy said he had been to the Co-operative store at Gateshead, and on returning to Newcastle saw the prisoner with an old man near the monumental masons at the High Level End. He saw her feel the old man's pockets and take his chain off his neck and his watch out of his pocket. When she had robbed the old man she left him and three men led him across the High Level Bridge after which they returned and joined the woman. She was remanded for a week to enable the police to find the old man who had lost his watch.

Newcastle Daily Chronicle, Tuesday September 10th, 1872

A very early photograph of the High Level Bridge, 1863. The monumental masons mentioned in the newspaper report were Walker, Emley and Beall who had their Newcastle showrooms on the approaches to the High Level Bridge. The walkway across the High Level Bridge was suitably dark and lonely for a robbery.

men do not appear in the collection of photographs.

The incidents described so far involve thefts in bars and the street rather than in brothels. Even the house where Phillis Robinson robbed Hunter was not strictly a brothel. A building could be properly styled a brothel if two or more prostitutes were using it to ply their trade. The women would contact their customers in the street, or more commonly in beer houses and inns, and take the men to the building. It would be very unusual to have a man-aged house for prostitutes with men calling to pay a 'Madame' for the service. The common practice was for a man or a woman to permit prostitutes to bring men to their premises and be paid a fee by the prostitutes each time. That was illegal – a risky business but lucrative. Between 1872 and 1873 there were not less than nine prosecutions in Newcastle upon Tyne for keeping brothels. Some of the keepers seemed to have no difficulty in paying

BROTHEL KEEPING

A woman named Martha Thompson alias Storey was yesterday fined £10 and costs for keeping a brothel in the High Bridge, Newcastle. The defendant immediately paid the money.

Newcastle Daily Chronicle, Friday July 4th, 1873

A view down High Bridge from Grey Street, around 1890. This was one of Newcastle's old narrow lanes.

the fines on the spot as may be seen in the following press report.

The going rate at this time seems to have been a fine of £10 or £20. The other streets covered in the prosecutions were Clayton Street West, Monk Street, Erick Street and Thornton Street. There were also two press reports regarding brothels at Back Row a notorious street that crops up regularly in prosecutions.

The reports reveal a curious similarity of Christian names, approximate

CONVICTION OF A BROTHEL KEEPER

A woman named Mary Jane Dawson was summoned before the Newcastle Magistrates on Tuesday (19th) for keeping a brothel at 22 Back Row, Newcastle. The facts of the case as stated by Superintendent Moore and Inspector Ellison were of a most revolting character and the magistrates inflicted a fine of £6 and costs.

Newcastle Courant, Friday March 22nd, 1872

NEWCASTLE POLICE CASES

At the Newcastle Police Court, yesterday before G.C. Atkinson and A. Potter Esqs., Mary Nugent, 18 years, charged with being the keeper of a brothel at No. 22 Back Row, was convicted of the offence and fined £10 or in default to be imprisoned for three months.

Newcastle Daily Chronicle, Saturday May 18th, 1872

ages and addresses.

According to the census of 1871, Mary Jane Dawson (an unmarried woman, 18 years of age and born in Northumberland) is recorded as a servant in Back Row, in the household of Margaret Smith a 28-year-old widow (no occupation recorded, born in Northumberland). Also present in the household was Eleanor, aged 6 years, daughter of Margaret Smith. There is no Mary Nugent in the house nor elsewhere in Back Row in the census. Did

Back Row crops up regularly in this book. It ran from Westgate Road towards St Nicholas' Church (now Cathedral). It was a squalid slum of lodging houses and tenements. The 1871 census confirmed gross over-crowding as there were 202 men, women and children living in the short street.

Mary Jane Dawson pass herself off as Mary Nugent to avoid heavier punishment for a second charge so soon after the other? Two convictions at the same household in two months show a reckless disregard for the consequences and the fines were not a deterrent. When the 1881 census was taken Mary Jane Dawson was serving a sentence in Newcastle Gaol, still unmarried but having with her in the prison her son Hugh, aged nine months.

The prosecutions were irregular and it is not clear if the police gave this offence low priority or whether there was no widespread problem and the police were merely responding to complaints. Stamping out the problem altogether was out of the question. Newcastle and Tyneside generally formed a major seaport. Seamen often feature in cases involving prostitutes and men came into the town from the countryside to seek out the women. Pressure from the police simply leads to displacement to other districts and towns. Achieving a significant reduction in the activities of prostitutes requires a sophisticated and long-term social strategy.

The Temperance Societies of the Victorian era took a close interest in prostitution as well as encouraging abstinence or at least the temperate use of alcohol. They saw the two problems as linked closely together. In 1854 the committee of the Newcastle upon Tyne Temperance Society published a document under the title *Newcastle As It Is, Reviewed in its Moral Aspects, Social State and Sanitary Condition.*

The authors claimed that a police report of 1838 revealed that at that time in the town there were 71 brothels and 31 houses where prostitutes lodged. They invited the reader to accept that these figures could be equated to a prostitute population of between 400 and 500. No corresponding figures or estimates were offered for the current year (1854). There is no denying the high demand for prostitutes and the readiness of women to take up that life in Newcastle as well as other major ports and cities around the United Kingdom. However, there is also a need to treat these figures with some caution. Totally reliable figures backed up by authentic research methods are simply not available.

The authors fixed the blame for this social problem firmly on drink, gambling and a lifestyle rooted in poverty. In particular they pointed to the numerous beer houses, inns, licensed music and dancing establishments as the haunt of prostitutes and men seeking them out. They were deeply concerned about the managers of these establishments having a vested interest in encouraging prostitution for the sake of the profits from sales to the men and women. Figures submitted to the Watch Committee in the mid-Victorian period show the annual returns for women charged by the police with drunkenness were 482 to the end of September 1863 and 475 to the end September 1867. So there was cause for concern. The Newcastle Watch Committee received complaints about brothels in 1876 (Erick Street, Carliol Square and the vicinity) and in 1876 and 1877 (Albion Street.)

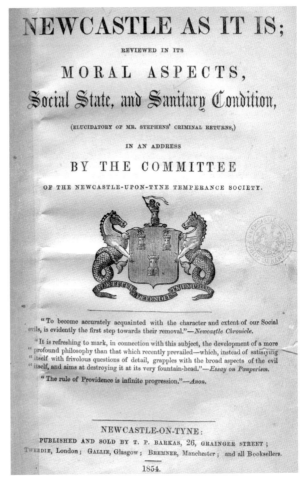

NEWCASTLE AS IT IS;

REVIEWED IN ITS

MORAL ASPECTS,

Social State, and Sanitary Condition,

(ELUCIDATORY OF MR. STEPHENS' CRIMINAL RETURNS,)

IN AN ADDRESS

BY THE COMMITTEE

OF THE NEWCASTLE-UPON-TYNE TEMPERANCE SOCIETY.

"To become accurately acquainted with the character and extent of our Social evils, is evidently the first step towards their removal."—*Newcastle Chronicle.*

"It is refreshing to mark, in connection with this subject, the development of a more "profound philosophy than that which recently prevailed—which, instead of satisfying "itself with frivolous questions of detail, grapples with the broad aspects of the evil "itself, and aims at destroying it at its very fountain-head."—*Essay on Pauperism.*

"The rule of Providence is infinite progression."—*Anon.*

NEWCASTLE-ON-TYNE:

PUBLISHED AND SOLD BY T. P. BARKAS, 26, GRAINGER STREET;
TWEEDIE, London; GALLIE, Glasgow; BREMNER, Manchester; and all Booksellers.

1854.

Thirty years later, in 1883, the same society published a long pamphlet on the same subject, this time with the title *The Devil's Mudbath or the Unholy Slave Traffic in Newcastle upon Tyne* by 'Citizen.' A copy of this, much-quoted, document at Newcastle City Library is endorsed in ink with the name 'John Hope' next to the word 'Citizen', however it is not clear who John Hope may have been.

The report of 1854 was reasonably measured and balanced in its tone but it is difficult at this distance in time to take the 1883 publication seriously. The rhetoric, hyperbole and high-flown language obscure the fact that the book contains little in the way of facts that can be checked, comparative statistics and corroboration. According to the author, Newcastle was awash with prostitutes and brothels in 1883. He asserted that a gentleman had been stopped by 32 different prostitutes as he walked the length of Grainger

Street from the station one evening. That would be equal to one prostitute every ten yards and is hard to accept. Elsewhere in the report on the subject of recruiting women into the trade he claimed to have it on reliable authority that 'the White Slave Market of Newcastle' was worse than the 'Slave Market of Zanzibar'!

There is much more in the same vein. However despite the book's extravagant language many sensible points were made. For example, as in the report of 1854, the author believed that the tolerance of the presence of prostitutes and their customers by the owners of bars, music halls and dancing salons encouraged prostitution. The publicans could not see beyond the profits they made from the women. There is a useful press report from that

A DISORDERLY HOUSE

At the Newcastle Police Court yesterday Jacob Carr, until recently landlord of the General Moore Inn, Barrack Road was fined ten shillings and costs for being drunk at his licensed premises on 14th April and £5 and costs for permitting drunkenness, and the conviction was ordered to be endorsed on his licence. The evidence went to show that on the night in question there were between 50 and 60 people – soldiers, civilians and prostitutes in the house, which was very disorderly. Mr Forster, who appeared on behalf of the defence, explained that the defendant had been previously convicted but that he had thereupon received notice to quit, which had now expired, and the defendant had left the house. He asked that the licence should not be endorsed, as it would be a great hardship upon the owner. The bench stuck to their decision.

Newcastle Daily Chronicle, Saturday 28th April, 1883

period that illustrates this point.

Failure to clear the highways of streetwalkers made it difficult for respectable women to pass without harassment. There was a deterrent and powers for the police to act against importuning under what was called the Town Police Clauses Act of 1847 Section 28 leading to fines or imprisonment up to 14 days.

Comment was also made on the importance of discouraging women from becoming prostitutes and helping those who wished to reform and give up the life. A penitentiary for that purpose was opened in Diana Street in the Victorian era. There was also the Brandling Home for Penitent Women. At the annual meeting of this establishment, held on 25th April 1883, it was reported that the average num-

Grainger Street in 1898.

ber of resident inmates in the past 12 months had been 16 from a total of 30 women taken in during the year. All of this indicates that there was a real problem to be dealt with.

A chaplain at the Newcastle Gaol apparently told the author that 84 out 90 women in the prison were prostitutes. In the 1871 and 1881 census returns for the prison none of the women are designated as prostitutes but the large majority of female prisoners were not shown as having an occupation of any kind.

The author pointed with admiration to Gateshead; because of intense activity by the police at that time the town was said to be clear of prostitutes and brothels. However he failed to recognise that at least part of the perceived increase at Newcastle must have been due to the former Gateshead prostitutes crossing the bridges to operate in Newcastle! The report was reviewed by only one local newspaper, the *Tyneside Echo*, and was not mentioned in the proceedings of the town council. The review in the *Tyneside Echo* in May 1883 was confined to short extracts from the pamphlet without editorial comment. A letter from 'Truth' in the same newspaper pleaded for more effective action to prevent women becoming prostitutes and also to rescue women from the awful trade.

Just three days after the report was published, a story appeared in a local paper underlining the extent of the problem:

A BROTHEL KEEPER SENT TO PRISON

At the Newcastle Police Court yesterday Matilda Clarke alias Brown, a well dressed woman, was charged with managing a brothel at 11 Stowell Square, the house was watched between 8.30 and 11.15 pm on Saturday, (28th April 1883) eighteen men each with a prostitute were admitted to the house by the defendant. Clarke on being charged said, 'I cannot help it.' The justices said they 'were determined to put a stop to this sort of thing,' and Clarke was sent to prison for six weeks with hard labour.

Newcastle Daily Chronicle, Wednesday May 9th, 1883

Similar reports can be found in the newspapers throughout 1883 and 'Citizen' used many of them to 'name and shame' the streets of Newcastle where brothels were located as a call for tougher action by the police and other authorities.

The *Borough Police Constable's Guide*, issued by the Newcastle Watch Committee to their force in 1869, drew attention to the power to arrest 'every prostitute wandering in the public streets or public highways, and behaving in a riotous or indecent manner' and also 'Obtain a knowledge of all reputed thieves and idle and disorderly persons.' Prostitutes fell into the category of idle and disorderly persons. However there was no official policy on dealing with prostitutes and the problem of brothels.

Of the 68 women in this collection of photographs 20 were described as prostitutes. Newcastle Gaol Statistics for the year ending September 1872 revealed that 110 prostitutes had been admitted to the gaol 230 times between them and admissions of prostitutes represented 36.4% of all female commitments to the gaol.

The link between the prostitute and street robbery was illustrated again in the case of Jane Cartner (alias Lockley and Hanley), another prostitute 'Well known to the police' as the local newspapers liked to report them.

Only 21 years of age at the time of her arrest, Cartner had a seven-year history of trouble with the police and the courts. Her list of 16 previous convictions reveals a 'tearaway' lifestyle in sharp contrast to the demure pose of her photograph. Three convictions for drunkenness and three for assaulting a constable set the scene. Beginning with wilful damage in 1866 at 14 years of age and ranging through prostitution, drunkenness, assault and thefts, Cartner's

Jane Cartner – doomed to a life of crime and imprisonment from her early teens.

criminal career led to her 17th appearance before the magistrates on 26th December 1872. It is interesting to note that in Victorian times courts tried cases even on Boxing Day.

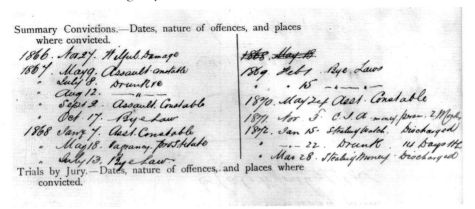

Jane Cartner's previous convictions listed on the reverse of her form.

Invariably cases like this began with the woman making contact with the man in a public house, and the couple leaving together to visit some quiet place or a house. Jane Cartner was released from prison on 25th May 1872, now aged 22 years, and having served the full six months imprisonment. There was no time off for good behaviour in those days. Her 18th conviction followed within 18 months.

Yet another example of the same style of theft by a prostitute but this time with male accomplices was Ann Wood alias Sweeney who was sent to prison for two months for stealing one and half (Victorian) pence. Wood was a 30-year-old (according to her prison form) married prostitute. It is not apparent in the photograph, but she was tattooed on her arms with shapes such as a heart and a cross and also a mixture of letters not forming words but probably initial letters for words; their meaning is not obvious. Wood had just one previous conviction, going back to June 1866, also for stealing from the person. On that occasion the magistrates simply discharged her after examination that usually meant that they thought no further action was required.

NEWCASTLE POLICE CASES

At the Newcastle Police Court before Mr Ald. Hunter and Mr Ald. Gregson:-

Ann Wood alias Sweeney 34 years of age, was charged with stealing three half-pence from a man named Edward Wilson while in a passage in Thornton Street about seven o'clock on Tuesday; while John Penty and George Scott 36 years of age were charged with being accomplices in the robbery. The three prisoners were further charged with frequenting the street for the purpose of committing felonies. The Bench after hearing the evidence of the man Wilson, PC John Smith and Sergeant Robert Anderson, sent the prisoners to gaol, the woman for two months and the two men for one month each.

Newcastle Daily Chronicle, Friday February 7th, 1873

Here again is an example of a prostitute shadowed by male accomplices working towards stealing money from what were known as 'punters'. This time all the thieves achieved was a paltry sum, but they had taken an enormous risk to get it; there was a police station at the corner of Thornton Street and Westgate Road!

Ann Wood.

A similar, and in some ways a pathetic, case was that of a 35-year-old Irish charwoman, Ann Kirk.

ALLEGED ROBBERY AT NEWCASTLE

At the Newcastle Police Court yesterday before Mr Ald. Pollard and Mr G.E. Atkinson, Ann Kirk was charged with stealing £1 5s 0d from William Henry Hill in a house in Fenkle Street about twenty past eleven o'clock on Thursday night, and James Newton was charged with being an accomplice in the robbery. The prisoners are well known to the police. After hearing the evidence of the prosecutor and a witness, the magistrates remanded the prisoners for a week.

Newcastle Daily Chronicle, Saturday February 8th, 1873

Ann Kirk's long history of previous convictions included trying to drown herself in May 1864. On this occasion, her 16th conviction, she was sent to prison for three months.

Finally on this subject of prostitutes, a tale that does not include women pictured in this collection but comes from the same period. It demonstrates so clearly the extraordinary lengths and risks they would take to steal as much as possible from their clients.

Ann Kirk.

ASSAULT AND ROBBERY IN NEWCASTLE

Yesterday at the Newcastle Police Court before Aldermen Dodds and Hunter, a woman named Mary Heads alias M'Larance and a girl named Jane Codling were charged with having stolen a quantity of wearing apparel, a pair of gold earrings and £3 in money, from a seaman named George Lemins. It appeared from the evidence that Lemins went into a house in Back Row where the prisoners lived, on the night of the 10th March. After staying in a room for sometime the prisoners, assisted by some men, stripped him of his clothes and left him almost naked. They also robbed him of a pair of ...

... gold earrings and his money, which amounted to £3. He was turned out of the house at 11 o'clock at night and he remained on the stairs until the following morning when he gave information to a policeman who happened to be passing. He assigned as a reason for staying on the stairs all night, that he was afraid to leave lest he would not find the house again as he was a perfect stranger to the town. When he was discovered by the policeman he was almost naked. The prisoners were each sent to prison for six months.

Newcastle Daily Journal, Tuesday March 18th, 1873

The Black Bull's Head on Westgate Street around 1890. This sort of squalid inn was the backdrop for many of the cases described in this chapter.

Stop thief!

One of the enduring images of Victorian and Edwardian costume is a man wearing a waistcoat with a gold or silver pocket watch and matching chains draped across from pocket to pocket.

It seems likely that the quality of the watch was an indicator of the standing of the owner in his community. However, even the most casual study of the men and women in this collection and others in contemporary records shows that the gentlemen's pocket watch, whatever its quality, was an irresistible target for the Victorian pickpocket.

The two brothers John Duffy, a labourer aged 16, and Peter Duffy, a bolt maker aged 20, and their friend George Lamb, a cart man, were not the most astute robbers in the Newcastle underworld.

A successful man showed his wealth with a tempting gold or silver fob watch and chain. Here the famous Tyneside rower James Renforth and his crew pose wearing theirs in 1871.

Brothers John (left) and Peter Duffy.

IMPUDENT ROBBERY IN NEWCASTLE

At the Newcastle Police Court on Monday two brothers named Peter and John Duffy were charged with assaulting a young man named John Davis; and stealing from him a silver watch, a gold Albert, a sealskin cap, and a silk pocket handkerchief, valued in all at £5 10s 0d and £2 in money. [Davis] was passing along Low Friar Street on Saturday night, at eleven o'clock when he was attacked by a number of young men, the prisoners being among the gang. He was seized by the throat, struck in the face; and in consequence of the rough usage and loss of blood he had suffered severely. The prisoners were most active in the assault and robbery. The evidence clearly connected the prisoners with the affair, and they were remanded.

Newcastle Courant, Friday November 15th, 1872

At the trial Lamb was sentenced to four months hard labour, and the other two to six months.

What possessed the Duffy gang to rob a man in Low Friar Street? The Duffys committed the crime on their own doorstep. The family home was at 25 Low Friar Street where they lived with their widowed mother Sarah, aged 60, and sister Margaret aged 21. According to the census there appears to have been multiple occupancy of houses in this street. Number 25 had 8 households comprising of 36 men, women and children.

John Duffy and George Lamb had no previous convictions. Peter Duffy, on the other hand had five convictions going back to 1867 (aged 15) for theft (3) and other offences with imprisonment and hard labour each time.

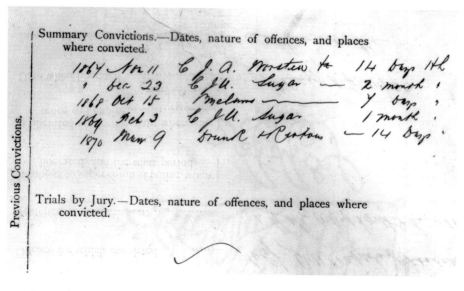

According to the newspaper report the Duffy brothers 'were most active in the assault and robbery' so it was only to be expected that they would receive a longer sentence than Lamb. The only surprising thing is that the magistrates did not commit all three for trial at the Newcastle Assizes charged with robbery with violence. Peter Duffy in particular would have faced serious consequences at such a trial.

The traditional cry of 'Stop Thief!' was actually heard in Victorian times on several chases through the streets of Newcastle although it was not reported for anyone in this collection. However, other examples vividly describe typical hot pursuit of thieves.

According to the evidence, O'Neill approached Melville and asked what time it was. Before he could give an answer, O'Neill snatched the watch and ran away. Melville followed, shouting, 'Stop thief'. He was joined by a policeman who was on duty in Grey Street but he had to give up after a short distance. Another policeman, who was on duty at the end of High Bridge, eventually caught O'Neill. When Melville described the theft, O'Neill claimed he was running to catch a train. The magistrates discovered that O'Neill had only recently been released from prison so committed him to be tried at the sessions. He was sentenced to ten years' penal servitude for the theft of the watch.

Dickinson shouted, 'Stop thief', and two passers-by, John Good and Charles Alexander McGregor, gave chase and ultimately stopped Stewart in Waterloo Street, beside St John's School. A policeman then took him into custody. During the chase, Stewart dropped the watch and guard; they were picked up by McGregor.

Stewart gave up a lot of his liberty for the sake of Mr Dickinson's watch. On 18th July 1873, exactly two weeks after the offence, Stewart appeared at the Newcastle Assizes and the judge sent him to prison for five years penal servitude.

No doubt the cry 'Stop thief' could be heard loud and clear in High Bridge on 12 September 1873 on the night that William Donnison was taking the air at his front door.

ROBBERY FROM THE PERSON IN DENTON CHARE.

William Badger (20) was charged before the Newcastle Magistrates yesterday morning with stealing a lever watch from the person of William Donnison on Sunday night last. [Donnison] was standing at his own door in Denton Chare at seven o'clock on Sunday night when the prisoner passed and snatched his watch from his pocket, and ran off with it.

Newcastle Daily Chronicle, Friday September 13th, 1872

Badger was recognised from Donnison's description and was taken into custody. He had only been out of prison a few days. He pleaded guilty and was sentenced to six months hard labour.

Although Badger had recently been in prison, press reports show that he had not been convicted of any offence on that occasion.

William Badger, a shoemaker and petty thief.

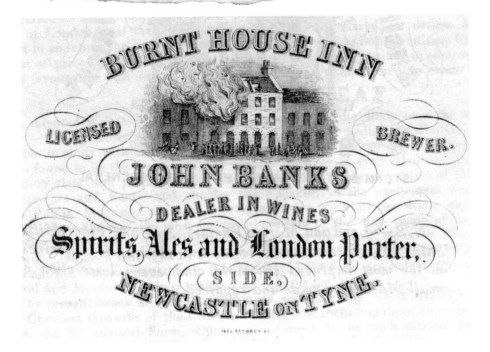

They were remanded in custody, but when the case came to trial there was insufficient evidence to convict them and they were discharged.

This young man, William Badger, recorded on his prison form as 20 years of age and a shoemaker by trade, had convictions going back to 1870 including four sentences of imprisonment. His victim, William Donnison, was, according to the census of 1871, a 61-year-old widower, a general dealer then living alone at 23, High Bridge.

There was nothing skilled or planned about street robberies and some perpetrators were confident about committing their crimes in apparently foolhardy locations.

Thomas Dixon, fireman, left, and John Allan.

Thomas Dixon and John Allan were each sentenced to be imprisoned for six months for assaulting Mr Jonah Bulman, cart proprietor, and stealing 5s 0d., from him in Carliol Street about a quarter to ten o'clock on the night of the 28th January.

Newcastle Daily Chronicle, Friday February 7th, 1873

Carliol Street was a gently sloping street leading north directly from the wall of Newcastle Gaol in Carliol Square (see the map on page 4 and the picture on page 37).

John Allan was a labourer, aged 19, born at Wark, with no previous convictions. His accomplice, Thomas Dixon was a 20-year-old fireman, from Newcastle. He had two previous convictions in 1870, one for stealing a gold watch – three months hard labour – the other for stealing gold brooches leading to six months hard labour.

In the same month an 'expert thief' came into town from Ireland or

Scotland. John Divine was smarter and better groomed than most of the people in this collection. On his prison form he is recorded as 17 years of age, born in Ireland, a guilder and carver with no known criminal history. None of this personal information could be corroborated or relied on.

The rather dapper John Divine, an 'expert thief'.

A young man named John Divine was charged with stealing a purse containing £1 4s 6d from the satchel bag of a lady named Jane Cole in the Butter Market about a quarter to twelve o'clock on Saturday forenoon.

Newcastle Daily Chronicle, Tuesday February 18th, 1873

In evidence, Detective Officer Martin stated that he saw the prisoner follow the lady in the market. While she was looking at some butter, Divine stood beside her, deliberately opened her bag and took out her purse. At his arrest Divine claimed that he had come from Belfast, but at the trial he changed his story, and said that he was a carver and guilder who had come from Edinburgh to seek work. He pleaded guilty to the charge and was sent to gaol for six months.

According to the report of the case in the *Newcastle Daily Journal*, the same day, 'Mr Superintendent Moore said he was quite satisfied that the prisoner was an expert thief, and he was only sorry that he had not had time to discover his antecedents.'

In the crimes examined so far in this chapter the criminal and the victim had no contact before the crime. But there are other examples where this was not the case.

In 1871, at the time of the census, Catherine Flynn alias Elizabeth Nolan aged 30, with no occupation recorded, was living at Dog Leap Terrace (possibly Dog Leap Stairs), Newcastle, with her husband John Flynn aged 29, a labourer and her daughter Mary aged four. The Flynns were one of the many Irish immigrant families in the town at that time. She had no court record, and we don't know why she started committing crimes, but within a few months she became a prostitute who targeted drunken men to steal their watches and whatever else might be available.

Catherine Flynn. Poverty may well have been the reason that forced her into a life of crime.

Flynn was convicted on 22nd July 1872 of stealing money from the person and the magistrates sent her to the Newcastle Gaol for 21 days with hard labour. Eight months later she appeared before the courts again for a similar offence. She is recorded on her prison form as 34-year-old married hawker from Ireland.

A woman named Catherine Flynn alias Elizabeth Nolan, was committed to prison for three months at the Newcastle Police Court, on Monday, on a charge of having stolen a sealskin purse from the person of George Foy, a recruiting sergeant for the Royal Marines, while in the Golden Lion Yard on Saturday night.

Newcastle Courant, Friday March 21st, 1873

Side around 1880. Dog Leap Stairs lead from the foot of Side up to the Castle Garth. Catherine Flynn robbed William Jackson of a silver watch in the Side.

Flynn was released from prison on 21st June 1873 and about six weeks later is before the Police Court again for stealing from the person.

Catherine Flynn, a middle-aged woman, was sentenced to three months imprisonment by the Newcastle Magistrates on Thursday morning for stealing a silver watch and guard from the person of William Jackson whilst in the Side. The prisoner was caught in the act of offering the articles for pledge at the shop of Mr Goolden, pawnbroker, yesterday, and on being taxed with the offence she admitted her guilt.

Newcastle Courant, Friday August 1st, 1873

Mary Ann McCasfrey, a 41-year-old married woman, was also recorded as a hawker but clearly worked as a prostitute. She was incorrectly reported as McCaffrey or McGafferty.

GOLD WATCH ROBBERY IN NEWCASTLE

A woman named Mary Ann McCaffrey was brought before Mr G.C. Atkinson and Mr A. Potter at the Manors Police Court charged with stealing from James Clarkson, landlord of the Engineers Arms public house, Sycamore Street, a gold chronometer watch with appendages valued at £60, in Renwick's Yard, Groat Market, on the afternoon of Saturday 21st December last ... The evidence showed that [Clarkson], who was not perfectly sober at the time, went from Renwick's bar into the yard about a quarter past three o'clock on the afternoon in question ...

Newcastle Daily Chronicle, Saturday April 19th, 1873

The evidence goes on to state that while Clarkson was in the yard a woman approached him three times, but Clarkson pushed her away. As he was going back to the bar, the woman pushed him into a corner by the entrance. Clarkson told her to go away but immediately after she left him he realised his watch was missing. A young girl named Ann Dobbs, who lived in Ridley Court, identified (McCasfrey) as the woman who pushed (Clarkson), and said she saw her go away from him with something in her hand.

The incident was also reported by a rival newspaper. The reporter had obviously mis-heard the prisoner's name, and was somewhat less tactful in describing the condition of Mr Clarkson.

THEFT OF A CHRONOMETER IN NEWCASTLE

Yesterday, a woman named Mary Ann McGafferty (45), was charged before Mr Atkinson and Mr Potter with having stolen a gold chronometer watch and appendages valued at £60 from Thomas Clarkson, whilst in state of intoxication in Renwick's Bar, Groat Market on 21st December 1872. The prosecutor is landlord of the Engineer's Arms, Sycamore Street. He met the prisoner in Renwick's Bar and after a short conversation with her he missed his watch but not until the woman had gone away. PC John Smith apprehended the prisoner in Pilgrim Street on Wednesday last and the watch, which had been pawned, was recovered. The prisoner pleaded guilty and was sentenced to four months imprisonment.

Newcastle Daily Journal, Saturday April 19th, 1873

This was another example of thieves using the town's pawnbrokers to raise cash on stolen goods. The pawnbroker's name in this case was Summerfield.

The Central Railway Station at Newcastle upon Tyne was a popular haunt of pickpockets, particularly at peak periods when congestion provided cover for their activities.

The arrest of Roger Gilbert, George Bright and Catherine Bright (offenders not listed in these records) at the railway station in October 1872 provided some insight into their way of working.

SUSPECTED PERSONS IN NEWCASTLE

At the Newcastle Police Court yesterday (before Messrs G.C. Atkinson and G.C. Potter) Roger Gilbert, 22, George Bright, 29, and Catherine Bright, 36 years of age, were charged with attempting to pick pockets at the Central Station about six o'clock on Tuesday night. The prisoners were also further charged with frequenting the station for the purpose of committing felonies the same night. Robert Bolton, the clever amateur detective, and Detective Officer W. Ritchie, were examined as witnesses and it appeared from their statements that the male prisoners, each of whom had a top coat over his arm, attempted to pick the pockets of several ladies and in each case the female prisoner was standing near them keeping a look out. Ritchie added that a great many pockets were picked the night before at the station. Mr Superintendent Moore said that Gilbert described himself as cheesemonger belonging to Hull, and the two Brights said they belonged to Glasgow. The Bench sentenced the prisoners to two months hard labour each.

Newcastle Daily Chronicle, Friday November 1st, 1872

At the same sitting of the Newcastle magistrates on Thursday 31st October 1872 appeared Richard Bradshaw and Agnes Stewart. Richard Bradshaw, alias Allan, was a thick set and bearded 40-year-old hawker from Ireland with several previous convictions and imprisonment. His crimes included assaulting a constable, stealing money from the person and being a rogue and vagabond. Agnes Stewart, alias Houghton, was a 28-year-old married hawker from Edinburgh, also with previous convictions; six months

The Central Station around 1863. The main entrance to the station and the first class refreshment room are behind and to the right of the train which stands in the dead-end bay used for the Edinburgh trains. At this time there were about 170 train arrivals and departures each day and about 35,000-40,000 passengers used the station daily. In 1866 the depth of the platforms was increased.

Agnes Stewart and Richard Bradshaw.

hard labour at the Newcastle Quarter Sessions in October 1869 for stealing a watch from the person and the same punishment from the Police Court in 1871 for stealing money from the person. There is an error on her prison form giving the date of conviction as 1873 instead of 1872. These two experienced thieves were picked up at the end of Neville Street at Newcastle upon Tyne in October 1872 loitering and stealing.

A woman named Agnes Stewart and man named Richard Bradshaw were charged with stealing a purse containing £6 from the person of Heinrich Lehmann in the neighbourhood of the Cattle Market on the night of the 18th October. The female was further charged with being found in Neville Street for the purpose of committing felonies on Wednesday night last. The magistrates after hearing the evidence against the prisoners sentenced them to six months hard labour.

Newcastle Daily Chronicle, Friday November 1st, 1872

They were released from prison on 30th April 1873 but had not reformed; a couple of months later they were caught loitering at the Central Station 'for the purpose of committing felonies,' which this time brought each of them another three months hard labour in the Newcastle Gaol.

To end this chapter here is a short but interesting story of how George Robb, a 19-year-old joiner from Scotland with no convictions, discovered that the justice system at Newcastle upon Tyne could act with great speed when given the chance.

PICKING POCKETS AT NEWCASTLE

A young fellow named George Robb was on Tuesday charged before the Newcastle Magistrates with stealing a purse containing £6 17s 9d belonging to Mrs Margaret Fenwick in Pilgrim Street that morning. A witness named Thomas Richardson saw the prisoner take a purse from the bag [Mrs Fenwick] was carrying, and run into the Black House [in Carliol Square]. Witness followed him, and the prisoner finding he had no chance of making his escape, pulled the purse out of his pocket. To avoid being committed for trial he pleaded guilty and was sentenced to six months imprisonment with hard labour.

Newcastle Courant, Friday November 1st, 1872

From his arrest for stealing in Pilgrim Street, to the Manors Police Station for charging, to the Manors Police Court for sentence, it took only a few hours for Robb to arrive at Newcastle Gaol in Carliol Square, just a few yards from where he was arrested. Let's hope the shock gave him a salutary lesson.

The unfortunate George Robb. Definitely a case of ale house to gaol house.

Flogged with twelve stripes

There are 11 girls and 29 boys aged 17 years and under in this collection. The tough attitude of Victorian judges and magistrates towards young offenders is well demonstrated by the cases of the youngest boys, Henry Leonard Stephenson aged 12, born at Castle Eden, and his accomplice, Michael Clement Fisher aged 13, born at West Hartlepool.

These two young choir boys from St Mary's Church, Rye Hill, Newcastle, were said to be 'of respectable parents', and had no history of trouble with the law. However, in September 1872, the boys went on a spree which would earn them severe punishments.

Between 6th and 30th September, Stephenson and Fisher broke into three houses. From John Thomas Green they stole a violin case and other articles. Joseph Brown of 27 Terrace Place, the manager of the Gallowgate Baths, was relieved of a ring and other articles. Ninety coins and other articles were stolen from 19, Summerhill Street, the home of Morison Johnston, a corn factor in the Town Hall Buildings. In court the boys pleaded guilty. The lawyers representing them asked for 'merciful consideration'; all the stolen property had been returned, both boys came from respectable families and character witnesses had

Henry Leonard Stephenson, aged 12.

spoken well of them. Fisher's mother promised to send her boy to sea and the Recorder was assured that Stephenson would be sent to India to his father.

As in some modern-day juvenile cases, the media was given a share of the blame: 'The boys had really broken into these houses, not so much for the purpose of stealing property, as from an idea that they were doing heroic manly acts, having perhaps been reading the wrong books'. The novel *Jack Sheppard* by William Harrison Ainsworth, based on the life of Jack Sheppard the highwayman who was hanged in 16th November 1724, was singled out for mention.

Michael Clement Fisher, aged 13.

The Recorder said he had considered ordering them to be whipped 'but that would be a terrible degradation'. Instead he committed Fisher to four months imprisonment with hard labour, and Stephenson to two months imprisonment and each was to have a day's solitary confinement at the beginning and end of the term of imprisonment.

There are only three cases in this collection of people charged with breaking and entering various properties. Such cases were dealt with at the Quarter Sessions or the Assizes and attracted heavier penalties than were awarded to most of the thieves described here. However, there was public concern about such crimes and it is interesting to see a public warning published by the *Daily Chronicle* about housebreakings in the same area and at the same time Stephenson and Fisher were arrested for their misdeeds. The *modus operandi* or method of entering described, was in the tradition of *Oliver Twist*.

BURGLARIES IN NEWCASTLE

Several attempts, some of them successful, have during the last fort-night been made to forcibly enter various dwelling houses in the neighbourhood of Elswick Lane, Newcastle. It would appear that a well-organised gang of thieves are at present at large in the town, and the daring manner in which they pursue their unlawful opera-tions has caused no little alarm in the neighbourhood ... The police are well aware of the state of affairs and are on the alert, but have not succeeded in discovering any of the thieves. The officers ... blame those of the inhabitants who leave their houses any length of time, without giving notice at the police station of their intention to do so, as ... the police make it their duty to look especially after [such] property.

Newcastle Daily Chronicle, Tuesday September 10th, 1872

The report goes on to describe 'one of the most cool and daring rob-beries', perpetrated between Saturday night and Monday morning in a house in Summerhill Street. The occupier was away from home due to ill health. The thieves removed the framework and glass of a small pantry win-dow and apparently put a boy through the hole which was not wide enough for a man. The thieves must have been inside the house for several hours; every room 'had been thoroughly overhauled – not a drawer or closet escaped'. All their efforts had been concentrated on a large safe containing valuable documents, money and other articles. 'A small chest of joiner's tools belonging to the house had been 'requisitioned'' but the burglars could not open it. While they were working they helped themselves to a couple of dozen bottles of Bass beer which they found in the house. In the end, the burglars left the property, taking only some some small articles of jewellery.

The Recorder's words about whipping in the Stephenson/Fisher case were significant. Corporal punishment was commonplace for children and adults alike, and was not confined to serious offences. Flogging was carried out in prison, police stations or even in the court precincts.

Summerhill Street, scene of the robberies of 1872.

FLOGGING AT DURHAM

(Summary) Durham Magistrates ordered three boys, aged 12, to receive eight strokes of the birch rod each – two boys for stealing screws, nails and window fittings and the other boy for stealing rabbit traps. 'The punishment was duly inflicted by the police at the close of the court and the boys were set at liberty.'

Newcastle Daily Chronicle, Monday May 13th, 1872

PUNISHMENT OF JUVENILES

At the Newcastle Police Court yesterday Alexander Muscroft, Benjamin Fitzpatrick, John McGuiness, C. McColville, Thomas Smith, George Dale and Richard McCabe, all boys, charged with breaking into the storehouse of the Cricket Field, Bath Road, on Sunday the 6th inst., and stealing therefrom six bottles of brandy, two dozen bottles of soda water and other articles were ordered to be flogged with a birch rod.

Newcastle Courant, Friday July 18th, 1873

The children in the last two examples did not form part of this collection. None of the prisoners discussed in this book was sentenced to be flogged for the offence on their prison form, but here are three of them who had the experience of being whipped for previous offences as younger children.

James Darley (or Donneley) was born at Shotley Bridge and recorded on his prison form as 16 years of age. He appeared before the Newcastle magistrates on 9th January 1873 charged with stealing three shirts belonging to John Hill. The previous convictions brought to the attention of the bench began when he was 11 years old in 1868 and was given 'twelve stripes' (12 strokes with a birch rod) for stealing butter. That punishment seems to have kept him quiet for three years. In 1871 and 1872 he was discharged after examination for charges of theft, which means the justices felt no further action was required. But then in September 1872, now 15 years old, Darley was back again for stealing two pigeons and the justices committed him to prison for two months hard labour. He had only been out of prison for two months when he was convicted and imprisoned for stealing the shirts.

James Darley.

At the Newcastle Police Court yesterday a lad named Robert Charlton, 16 years of age, was sentenced to four months imprisonment for stealing two pairs of boots from the shop of Mr Chricherton, Grainger Street on Friday afternoon.

The Newcastle Daily Chronicle, Tuesday November 12th, 1872

Robert Charlton.

Just nine days earlier, the above 16-year-old Newcastle labourer had been released from prison after finishing two months hard labour for stealing pigeons. The previous year, 1871, Charlton had done seven days hard labour plus a flogging of twelve stripes for stealing 50 cigars.

The third example is Robert Scullion who was just 13 years of age when he came before the Newcastle Police Court on the 14th July 1873. Recorded as a labourer, standing four feet two inches high and a native of Newcastle, he was charged with stealing clothing. Six weeks earlier the same justices had ordered Scullion to be flogged, 'eleven stripes' with the birch rod for stealing a rabbit. Sterner action was inevitable on the second charge. Scullion was sentenced first to fourteen days hard labour then three years at Market Weighton Reformatory School.

Robert Scullion.

His accomplice Henry Miller, a boy of 14 born in Berwick, with no criminal history, was sent to the Newcastle Gaol for 14 days hard labour.

Sending Robert Scullion to the reformatory school at Market Weighton indicates that the boy was a Roman Catholic. The establishment was known as the Yorkshire Catholic Reformatory School for Boys, and was based at Holme-on-Spalding, Market Weighton, East Yorkshire. It was established in July 1856 for 225 boys. In 1933 it became the St William's Approved School for Roman Catholic Boys.

Henry Miller.

Girl offenders who were Catholics were sent from Newcastle to the Dalbeth Roman Catholic Reformatory School, Glasgow.

Jane Farrell was a girl aged 12, with no criminal history, who appeared before the Newcastle magistrates on 6th January 1873, charged with stealing two boots. Farrell was sentenced to ten days hard labour in the Newcastle Gaol. Her prison form is endorsed on discharge 'Removed to Dalbeth Reformatory, Glasgow'.

The Reformatory Schools were established by Act of Parliament in 1854 and according to Dr Robert Spence Watson, speaking at Newcastle Literary and Philosophical Society in 1884, 'In 1881 there were 42 Reformatory Schools for boys and 20 similar schools for girls in England and Scotland containing an aggregate 5,518 boys and 1,220 girls.'

Jane Farrell.

Dr Watson identified the problem with the legal requirement that a child should have served imprisonment before going to a reformatory.

The children who are upon the borderland which divides the criminal from the non-criminal class are not the objects of Reformatory work, – that presupposes actual and serious crime. A child must have been convicted of an offence punishable by imprisonment or penal servitude, and must have been sentenced to at least ten days' imprisonment before it is considered ripe for reform. That ten days imprisonment is a blot upon a valuable Act. When, as sometimes happens, the child is made the associate of hardened criminals, imprisonment is a strange preliminary to the remedial work which is to follow, and is out of keeping with the spirit of the legislation for criminal reform.

The establishment of Reformatory Schools in the North-East of the country stemmed from the formation of a high-powered committee on 27th October 1852 at the house of a Newcastle magistrate, Michael Longridge. At the head of this group were the Mayors of Newcastle and Gateshead, the Recorder, Town Clerk and Sheriff of Newcastle upon Tyne and many other magistrates and gentlemen of the area. On 17th December 1852 they published a 'Report of the Committee Appointed to Examine into the State of Juvenile Crime in Newcastle and Gateshead.'

The report is full of interesting facts and figures about juvenile crime of that period. In the year ending November 1852, the police at Newcastle apprehended 663 persons 17 years and younger (556 males and 107 females) compared with 314 in 1838 (236 males and 78 females). An increase of

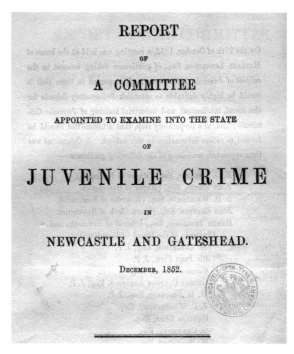

REPORT

OF

A COMMITTEE

APPOINTED TO EXAMINE INTO THE STATE

OF

JUVENILE CRIME

IN

NEWCASTLE AND GATESHEAD.

DECEMBER, 1852.

more than 100% over 14 years. There was a larger increase for the boys than the girls. The report then looked at the numbers committed to the Newcastle Gaol and concluded that in Newcastle an average of 663 juveniles were

Name.	Age when first Committed.	No. of years over which the register extends.	Number of Committals.	Final result recorded.
I. I.,	10	4	9	7 years' transportation.
E. C.,	11	2	9	Ditto.
I. G.,	13	4	12	Ditto.
I. P.,	10	4	12	Ditto.
M. F.,	9	5	13	Ditto.
M. D.,	8	5½	13	Ditto.
M. R.,	11	2	14	Ditto.
I. B.,	12	7½	16	Ditto.
I. I.,...	12	7	18	10 years' ditto.
W. C.,	10	4	19	12 months' imprisonment.
I. W.,	10	6	19	10 years' transportation.
I. L.,	12	6	19	Larceny—no bill.
N. L.,	9	6½	19	Burglary—15 years' transportation.
A. M.,	13	5	26	10 years' transportation.
T. F.,	9	9	29	Now in gaol for robbery with violence.

A chart from the report. Note the ages of the boys convicted.

arrested by the police each year. 264 of them went to prison and of them, 85 (one third) had served previous prison terms. Around 125 of the juvenile prisoners were claimed to be known thieves, who, it was predicted, would be transported within a few years.

Transportation was just ending at this time, so perhaps penal servitude should be substituted for transportation. Twenty years later the figures for children passing through the prison had considerably reduced. During the year ended 20th September 1872 99 boys and 15 girls had been committed to the gaol (37th Report of the Inspectors of Prisons).

The committee also looked at the correlation between juvenile crime and the increasing population of the town and concluded that juvenile crime was increasing four times as fast as the population, doubling in just 13 years. The number of habitual thieves had risen by 120%, in the same period.

The committee cited many examples to prove that poverty, overcrowding and alcoholism amongst parents and guardians were major causes for the great numbers of children passing through the hands of the police, the courts and the town gaol. They questioned the wisdom of whipping and imprisonment as instruments of reform.

The rather grim Netherton Training School around 1910. It started life as a group of farm buildings but by this date had expanded.

Samuel Thompson, Governor of the Gaol, (1836-1860) expressed his opinion of the effect of imprisonment in the following terms: 'I have rarely known a poor boy or girl, committed to this prison whether for a long or a short period who has not become a frequent inmate of its walls; and I am convinced that this must continue to be the case until some reformatories, such as are now, are established.'

It is hardly surprising that the committee recommended the establishment of a reformatory school on the 'Farm-school system' near Newcastle. The report pointed out that it was 'less costly to the country to reform a criminal than to leave him to run his course of crime'.

Over the next few years a reformatory was opened at Newcastle. By the end of the decade the North Eastern Reformatory School for Boys was set up at Netherton near Morpeth to take up to 100 boys. In 1933 the school became Netherton Training Approved School until it was closed in the 1970s. Non-Catholic girls were sent to a reformatory at Sunderland.

There was just one boy found in this collection of prison forms who was sent to the Reformatory at Netherton in the period December 1871 to December 1873.

John Reed had assembled quite a record for a boy of 15 years. Aged 11, he was flogged with 12 stripes of the birch in June 1870, and then followed four short prison sentences 1871-1873. He had already served seven days' hard labour on 6th February 1873 for a bye-law offence when he appeared at court again on the 25th February on a charge of 'assaulting Alexander Ridley and stealing 4s 0d., from him at the end of Back Row about eleven o'clock on Saturday night'. His accomplices were not in court. He was sentenced to gaol for 14 days and to a reformatory for five years. He was a fortunate boy to be given the chance to build a new life at the reformatory.

John Reed.

However, the reformatory system was not always a success; tucked away in these records are three 'old boys' who reverted to their criminal ways.

Robert Bolam, a 20-year-old labourer, born in Gateshead. In 1865, aged 13, he had been flogged for stealing. In 1869 aged 16 or 17 he was convicted of stealing lead, served 14 days hard labour then went to the reformatory at Netherton. Three years later, on 3rd September 1872, probably on licence from Netherton, Bolam again appears before the Newcastle Court for stealing clothing with two accomplices, William Salmon and Thomas Garratty. All three were sent to

Robert Bolam.

prison for six months' hard labour.

The second example, John Grieveson, went to prison for 14 days on 26th October 1866 then to Netherton Reformatory School for four years for stealing money. Seven years later, aged 21, he succumbed to an opportunist theft following a fire. Grieveson pleaded guilty, and was committed for four months. At the trial it was stated that this was Grieveson's third appearance before the magistrates and his last conviction was for 14 days. However his prison form shows only one previous conviction – the one that sent him to Netherton.

John Grieveson.

THEFT OF PIGEONS AT A FIRE.

Yesterday at the Newcastle Police Court before Aldermen Bell, Hedley and Pollard, two young men named Henry Hedley and John Grieveson were charged with having stolen thirty pigeons, the property of Walter Charles Bulman. It appeared from the evidence that the pigeons were in a dovecote above the stables of Mr Bulman, carter, Erick Street. A fire broke out on the adjoining premises on Friday night at eleven o'clock and during its progress … Grieveson was seen on the roof near the dovecote, which was broken open, and the pigeons stolen. Six of the pigeons were afterwards found in the possession of the prisoner Hedley, who got them from the prisoner Grieveson.

Newcastle Daily Journal Tuesday February 25th, 1873

Hedley was discharged as the magistrates believed that he had no idea the pigeons were stolen.

It is a similar story for Joshua Robson, right. On 23rd November 1866, aged just 12, he was sentenced to ten days hard labour followed by five years at Netherton. By coincidence Robson was at the reformatory at the same time as John Grieveson and their trials for re-offending were held on the same day.

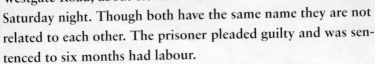

A young man named Joshua Robson, was charged with stealing 20s 0d., from the desk of Mr Joshua Robson, butcher, Westgate Road, about eleven o'clock on Saturday night. Though both have the same name they are not related to each other. The prisoner pleaded guilty and was sentenced to six months had labour.

Newcastle Daily Journal, Tuesday February 25th, 1873

Although the reformatory system did not work for all young thieves, the authorities tracked the behaviour of inmates for a few years after discharge and the figures showed that on the whole good results had been achieved. The Governors of the North Eastern Reformatory met annually. In 1873 they heard that of the 111 boys who had left the reformatory in 1869, 1870 and 1871, three had died, 81 were in employment and doing well. Eleven were of doubtful character, 12 convicted of crime, and four unknown.

According to the report, the number of inmates had risen from 148 to 151 over the year. Fifteen boys from Newcastle were admitted that year, along with one from Northumberland, 22 from County Durham, seven from other counties. One boy was re-admitted after absconding. Nearly all of them had been convicted more than once. Boys who had completed half their term of detention were sent out to work on licence and this system was working satisfactorily. The governors heard that the discipline of the Reformatory had been well maintained, there had been few attempts to abscond, and the general health of the inmates had been exceedingly good.

The Victorians were well aware of the problems of destitute young people and provided other philanthropic schemes to deal with them. Reformatory Schools should not be confused with 'Ragged Schools' and 'Industrial Schools'. Ragged Schools provided refuge and education for destitute youngsters. Newcastle upon Tyne had a Ragged School in Garth Heads at the beginning of New Road. In 1859 this establishment was certified for use also as an Industrial School which had a wider remit. Under the Industrial Schools Acts of 1859 and 1851 courts could send vagrant children to the Industrial Schools for education, trade training and to introduce the young people to a disciplined living regime.

In the 1871 census the 'Ragged and Industrial Schools' at Garth Heads, Newcastle provided a home for 59 boys aged eight to 16 years, and 43 girls aged seven years to 16 years, a total of 102. The school was run by Superintendent Ralph Willoughby (32 years old and born at Alnwick)who lived there with his family. There were four female staff and a male warden called John Fawcett.

Another initiative to help young people was to form 'Shoeblack Brigades' in the towns and cities. Various philanthropists around the country seem to have been credited with starting up these groups including Lord Shaftesbury, Quinton Hogg and William Quarrier of Glasgow.

A paperboy posed for the camera around 1880.

The idea was to organise a group of needy children into a uniformed brigade of shoeblacks, then put them at key points, such as railway stations. In this way they could earn money to support themselves and avoid a life of idleness. The purpose of the uniform was to reassure the public that these were legitimate young people providing a service and not a band of beggars. In London the uniforms were scarlet in other places they were brown.

Dr Robert Spence Watson was a distinguished citizen of Newcastle, a businessman, a liberal, philanthropist, deeply involved in public affairs (particularly education), secretary of the Ragged Schools for many years and President of the Literary and Philosophical Society among many other things. He was appointed a Privy Counsellor in later life. Dr Watson, despite his busy life, found time to organise a 'Shoeblack Brigade' at Newcastle. In a lecture to the Literary and Philosophical Society in 1884, he described the successful conversion of a boy going wrong in around 1858.

I led the management of the Newcastle Shoeblack Brigade, we captured one lad about ten years of age, who had been thrice convicted and punished at the Assizes and had undergone six months imprisonment in Durham Gaol for burglary. In the true sense he was not a bad lad; quick to learn, contented, smart, obedient (when we had once come to a mutual understanding), he is now a man thirty-five years of age, an honest and upright member of society, instead of a returned convict under the supervision of the police.

Next door to the police headquarters in Manors was the home for the Newcastle Shoeblack Brigade. The census of 1871 lists the establishment as 'Manors Shoe Black Home'. Patrick W. Markham, a 33-year-old Irishman was Superintendent. In addition to Markham's family 17 boys aged 12 to 17 years lived there. Six were listed as 'shoeblacks', four errand boys and the rest were apprenticed to various trades. Not listed as living there was the 19-year-old housebreaker and shoeblack Patrick O'Neill, whose story appears at the beginning of this book.

Very little survives in local archives about the shoeblacks but there is one note suggesting they may not always have behaved well. The Watch Committee Minutes for Newcastle contain a note on 6th October 1871: 'Letter from Hodgkin Barnett House. Letter read complaining of the conduct of the shoeblacks in front of the bank. Referred to the Chief Constable for his report.' Hodgkin, Barnett, Pease, Spence and Co. were bankers in St Nicholas Square, Newcastle upon Tyne. The minutes carry no record of a subsequent report from the Chief Constable.

It is clear that there was a problem of vagrancy, destitution and criminal behaviour among children in Victorian Newcastle. It was all too easy for boys to follow a path leading to crime and long-term detention and for girls to drift into prostitution. The courts could use a limited range of punishments for children – flogging and detention of one form or another. Although enlightened people like Samuel Thompson, Governor of the town gaol, recognised that imprisonment had a detrimental effect on children, the police, magistrates and prison authorities did not have the resources and flexible options of the services available in the 21st century. There was certainly the will to look at the best action for each individual to control and reform young offenders. Alternative strategies were emerging but there was still a long way to go.

Finally, here is the short story of Michael Dixon aged 16, who was not in the collection but serves to underline and emphasise how different things were back in the 1870s.

APPRENTICE SENT TO PRISON

At the Newcastle Police Court yesterday Michael Dixon, 16 years of age, an apprentice smith at Sir William Armstrong and Co.'s Works was sent to gaol for fourteen days, for absenting himself from his work without leave on 23rd December, this being his second offence.

Newcastle Daily Chronicle, Tuesday January 21st, 1873

Six months hard labour

The prison referred to throughout this book stood in Carliol Square, Newcastle from 1828 to 1925. It was known as the Newcastle Gaol and House of Correction until 1877 when control of prisons transferred to the Prison Commissioners; then it became HM Prison, Newcastle upon Tyne. Each one of the prisoners described in this collection of prison forms spent at least one sentence in this prison, anything from seven days to 15 months. Some men and women were in the prison on many occasions.

John Dobson, the famous Newcastle architect, designed the prison to follow the on-going practice of the 18th century. Each shire county and county borough had a secure building, a county or town gaol, to house prisoners awaiting trial, sentence and transportation; provision was also made for debtors. The 'prison' section of this establishment did not hold short-term prisoners and the long-term prisoners were transported. Prisoners serving short sentences with hard labour went to the House of Correction. It was common to have the two institutions in separate buildings in the 18th century. But in the great wave of building new prisons at the end of the century and into the next, prisons and correction houses were built together with a governor for the prison and a master for the correction house. The function of the correction house was to receive short sentence prisoners into secure and spartan accommodation, often beginning with a flogging, then put them to hard work usually for two weeks but sometimes up to six months. The objective was to try to instill the work ethic into the prisoners and remove them from an idle and vagabond life.

Dobson had designed a set of small prison blocks connected to a central service and observation block rather like spokes in a semi-circle. Within a decade or so his design was attracting criticism from the prison inspectorate formed in 1836. It seems that for good ventilation in the prison John Dobson fitted large holes above each cell door, which provided an inlet for air but an outlet for the prisoners to call out to each other as much as they wished. The first inspectors, Frederic Hill, followed by John Kincaid, asked for radical (and expensive) changes to stop communication and mixing of prisoners and to support the ideas of the time; separation and silence.

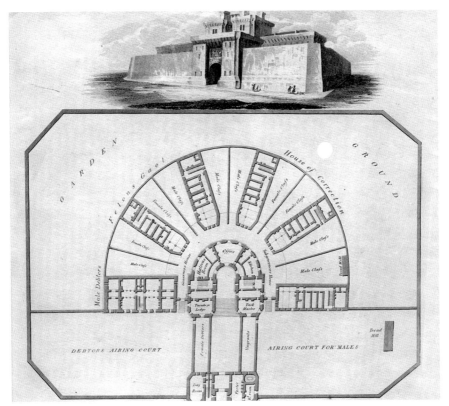

John Dobson's plan for his new gaol on Carliol Square, 1828. Only five of the designed six blocks were built.

Transportation ceased in the middle of the 19th century. The activities of the new police forces brought more offenders before the courts and into the gaols. The authorities began providing penitentiaries for long serving prisoners and the local gaols took the shorter sentence prisoners. The distinction between prisons and correction houses became blurred then disappeared altogether. At Newcastle the governor began to run everything without a master.

One man in the collection had experience of local prison and the penitentiary. Edward Shevlin alias Sherling, a labourer, 32 years of age was sent to the Newcastle Gaol for six months on 3rd September 1872 for stealing a coat.

Prison sentences of say three years and upwards at the Quarter Sessions or Assizes were often termed termed penal servitude and served in national prisons called penitentiaries. Edward Shevlin had two such sentences in his extensive record, the second being seven years at the Newcastle Quarter Sessions on 3rd January 1866 for stealing a coat. Shevlin and similar prisoners could get time off their sentence for good behaviour in the establishment and be released from the penitentiary early – on licence, as it was known. Shevlin breached the terms of his release on licence by the conviction of 1872 (again for stealing a coat). He served six months in the

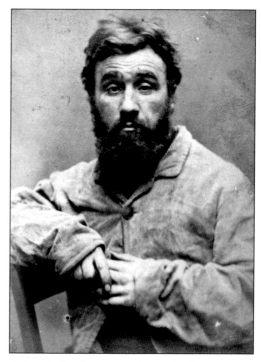

Edward Shevlin, a man in need of a coat.

Newcastle Gaol for the new offence, then the prison authorities returned him to the Millbank Penitentiary, London to serve out the remainder of his seven year sentence of 1866. His prison form was endorsed accordingly.

There was no similar licence or early release system in those days for summary sentences, that is to say convictions before the magistrates' courts.

The members of the Newcastle Town Council did not want to spend more money on their prison. Discussion of the prison inspectorate criticisms dragged on for more than twenty years. Newcastle upon Tyne suffered the indignity of being singled out annually in reports to the Secretary of State for the failings of the prison. John Kincaid always stressed that the prison building was the problem not the staff. He invariably complimented them. His report of 1857 included a heartfelt plea:

It appears to me that a young female convicted of a first offence might as well be committed to any seminary of vice in the town as to the female

prison of Newcastle, where she is forced to mingle with associates whose habits and conversations all tend to debase the mind and lead to an evil course of life. It is true they are under certain constraint and subject to punishments for breach of prison rules, but these are set at nought, for punishments in such a prison only serve to inflame the passions instead of correcting and subduing. It is also true they have the services of an able chaplain and efficient teachers, but it can only be considered a mockery of religion sending prisoners to chapel while they are obliged to return to such a den of vice as they now occupy. In short though no expense has been spared in supplying all the requirements of a prison, the prison itself is wanting, and until suitable accommodation is provided, all other appliances may be considered as so much thrown away.

(22nd Annual Report of the Inspectors of Prisons for the Northern District 1857)

Such criticisms continued. In February 1859 John Kincaid reported that generally the prisons in the district continued to be well managed and in excellent order. However Newcastle was again singled out for criticism.

The only marked exception, in a Prison of its class, is the Borough Gaol of Newcastle-on-Tyne, the confinements there being of a character more calculated to encourage vice and crime than to deter or to reclaim; and to the separate report on that Prison I again respectfully beg to direct your attention.

(24th Annual Report of the Inspector Prisons for the Northern District 1859)

In the summer of 1860 the Town Council came to terms with what had to be done and work began on major changes to the cells of the prison. The radial prison blocks were pulled down and a long prison block, also designed by John Dobson, was erected parallel to the back wall of the prison. The prison remained like that until it was closed and demolished in 1925. The council members at Newcastle upon Tyne must have been relieved to have much more satisfactory inspectorate reports thereafter.

Thomas Robins was the prison governor in the period covered by this collection of prison forms, 1871-1873. He had been in charge of the gaol since 12th April 1860. Before that he had been Governor of the West Riding

HM Prison, Carliol Square, around 1924, shortly before it was demolished.

of Yorkshire Reformatory School at Mitford.

The census of 2nd April 1871 records that the gaol housed Thomas Robins (born at Malmesbury, Wiltshire and now aged 56) and his family, the Deputy Governor Joseph Little and his family, plus 20 other members of staff and families. A total of 150 prisoners were detained in the prison (123 men and 27 women). No distinction was made in the census return between debtors, convicted prisoners and remand prisoners. The ages ranged between 14 and 73 for the male prisoners and 11 and 51 for females. There were no names for the prisoners just their initials. Of five male prisoners under 17, the youngest, initials P.C., was 14 years old, a labourer born at Lancaster. There were two female prisoners under 17 – E. McD aged 11, born at Warwick, and M.J.W. aged 13, a domestic servant, born at Newcastle. Twenty-six prisoners (17.3%) claimed to be born in Scotland, 22 (14.6%) in Ireland and 53 (35.3%) at Newcastle upon Tyne. The remaining 49 (32.8%) were born elsewhere.

Although the prisoner population on census day was 150, around 2,000 prisoners moved in and out of the prison each year. According to inspectorate reports an average of 192 criminals (143 males and 49 females) were in custody each day in 1871 – rather more than shown on the census return. There must have been many short sentence prisoners passing through. One thousand and eighty males were sentenced that year, and of those 698 (about 64%) were serving one month or less. Of 691 females sentenced, 509

Carliol Square Prison, 1925.

(about 74%) were serving one month or less. These figures followed national trends for summary convictions and sentences.

After the substantial changes of the early 1860s Newcastle Gaol had 173 male cells and 81 female cells. This meant that in the early 1870s, the prison staff could comfortably handle the numbers passing through the establishment.

The Prisons Inspector in this decade was T. Folliott Powell who reported for the year 1873 that there were two classes of hard labour at the Newcastle Gaol.

Hard labour of the 1st class is carried out by the cranks, stone-breaking, chopping and beating rope, making mats and matting with heavy looms, and pumping water. At the cranks 12,000 and 14,000 revolutions is the

required daily task, and at the stone breaking 1¹/₂ cwt. (112 pounds) per hour for a day of six or more hours.

Hard labour of the 2nd class consists of weaving with light looms, making ships fenders and mats, carpentering, smith's work, tailoring, shoemaking, washing and cleaning.

(37th and 38th Annual Reports of the Inspectors of Prison for the Northern District 1873/4)

Sarah O'Reilly

A 'cranks' at Ruthin Gaol, Wales. This device contained heavy weights to be turned over on a spindle by a winder handle, a task often carried out in isolation.

The prison diet was an interesting exercise in the carrot and stick approach to punishment and discipline and one that surely stirred up discontent amongst the prisoners. For periods not exceeding 14 days male and female prisoners serving simple imprisonment – there appears to be just one in this collection: James Augustus Jobling (see page 20) – or hard labour 2nd class were fed a pint of gruel for breakfast, one pound of bread for dinner and a pint of gruel for supper. Prisoners working at hard labour 1st class were fed the same diet except on Fridays when they received a pint of soup with their bread for dinner.

The gruel was made of oatmeal and water. The soup mentioned here was much like a stew, the guidance quoted in the reports said 'The soup to contain per pint three ounces of fresh butchers meat, three ounces of potatoes, one ounce of barley, rice or oatmeal, half an ounce of peas, one ounce of onion or leeks, with pepper and salt.'

Longer periods in the gaol brought greater rations. After 12 months male and female prisoners working at hard labour 2nd class received for breakfast one pint of gruel and eight ounces of bread, for dinner (on four alternate days) four ounces of cooked meat without bone (but only three ounces for women), one pound of potatoes and eight ounces of bread or (on the other three alternate days each week) one pint of soup, half a pound of potatoes and eight ounces of bread; for supper one pint of gruel and eight ounces of bread. The same diet was given to men and women of 1st class hard labour except the gruel for breakfast was changed to a pint of cocoa every other day. All prisoners started on 1st class hard labour for the first month, the movement to the lighter 2nd class labour depended upon hard work and good behaviour.

Punishment for misbehaviour inside the gaol included change of diet – literally bread and water with a pound of bread for each meal for three days – after that offenders got one pint of gruel for breakfast, one pound of bread for dinner and one pint of gruel for supper. The restriction of diet punishment was used 370 times in 1873. This might be combined with solitary confinement or confinement in dark cells (used 22 times in the same year).

Going back some years to John Kincaid's report for the year 1855 there is a very interesting note on the 176 'other punishments' used that year. All but two were shower baths, which, according to the Governor, formed a 'very efficacious punishment which he could scarcely do without'. The exceptions were used in 'two instances of gross misconduct by two females violently shouting calling out from their dormitories, and disturbing the whole prison, when a headpiece or muzzle was placed upon the prisoners, which effectually prevents them from shouting but allows them to respire freely'.

The device described here is an old fashioned restraint for gossiping women called 'the branks.' Newcastle once had three of these devices; one survives in local collections to this day. It was an open helmet of metal strips, hinged so that it could be fitted over a woman's head. When closed it forced a strip of flat metal, sometimes sharp, into her mouth over the tongue to keep it still. Use of this device was not mentioned in any of the other inspection reports.

Kincaid commented that suitable accommodation for the prisoners would avoid 'obliging the governor to resort to punishments, which are not authorised by the prison rules.'

Punishments ordered by the court, such as flogging might take place, in the prison. High Court Judge Baron Piggot passed comment on flogging at the Newcastle Assizes in December 1871 in relation to a charge of robbery with violence 'The law provides a very severe punishment for this particular crime, a special punishment, a punishment of flogging and although that is a punishment which is resorted to with great reluctance it has a good effect in repressing this species of crime.'

The punishment ordered by Judge Baron Piggot on that occasion was described in the Newcastle upon Tyne Town Council Minutes 1871/1872.

11th January 1872. The punishment of flogging with cat-o'-nine-tails was inflicted in Newcastle Gaol this morning, upon a prisoner named John Smith. He was convicted at the last Newcastle Assizes, held on 13th December 1871, before Mr Baron Piggot, of a garotte robbery in Newgate Street, and was sentenced to four years penal servitude, and also to receive eighteen cuts with the cat-o'-nine-tails. The administration of the flogging was witnessed by the Mayor (Mr T.L. Gregson) as the chief magistrate of the town; the Sheriff (Mr J.L. Falconar); Messrs Ralph Cook; C. Smith; R. Cail Stokoe; G. Gibson and G. Stewart, members of the Gaol and Watch Committee of the Corporation; Mr Robins, Governor of the Prison, and R. Little the Deputy Governor; Mr Hardcastle, the Surgeon to the Prison, Mr Joseph Davison (Sheriff's Officer) and two medical students. The instrument employed on this occasion was a regulation 'cat', having been expressly sent from the Home Office for the purpose.

Prisoners serving less than one month slept on plank beds without mattresses. Depending on their length of sentence, other prisoners might be granted a mattress if they behaved well and worked very hard. There was a chaplain who read prayers daily in the prison chapel and conducted two services each Sunday, Good Friday and Christmas Day. Dr Hardcastle, a well-known local doctor, was the prison surgeon and called daily.

One of the prisoners in this collection had an unusual previous conviction on his form. His name was William Bell. He was a 33-year-old married blacksmith, sent to prison in September 1872 for six months with hard labour for theft.

STEALING BEEF

Yesterday William Bell 33 years of age, was sentenced by the Newcastle Magistrates to be imprisoned for six months for stealing a piece of beef valued at 5s 6d from the shop of Mr Michael Blenkinsop, Butcher Market on Saturday night, there being several convictions against him.

Newcastle Daily Chronicle, Tuesday September 17th, 1872

Bell had been in trouble with the police constantly over the previous 16 years and had accumulated eight convictions. He was committed to the Newcastle Gaol on 20th May 1857 for two months hard labour for being a rogue and vagabond. He was released on 20th July 1857. Four days later he was back at the Newcastle Police Court charged with 'Attempting to throw tobacco into the gaol.' For this he was sentenced to one month hard labour.

Security was a constant problem at the gaol. Bell's case reveals how easy it was to throw anything into the prison yards. The following year John Kincaid reported a similar experience at the gaol.

In one of my visits to the gaol during the past year I had an opportunity of witnessing the manner in which forbidden things are passed into the prison. Accompanied by the head warder, I was examining a piece of ground between the boundary wall and the end of one of the prison wings, when all at once, on some understood signal, a regular heavy shower of missiles commenced flying over my head, some from the prison yard, but the greater from beyond the boundary wall; most of these from the outside reached their destination, but a great many others missed their mark, and striking against the wall of the prison wing, fell near where we were standing. I picked up one parcel containing about a pound of tobacco, and it was written on the cover that a similar quantity would be thrown over on the Saturday following. The missiles thrown from the prison were chiefly pieces of bread, which probably conveyed some communication; 'the shower' lasted about five minutes.

(24th Annual Report of the Inspectors of Prisons for the Northern District 1859)

The changes to the prison of 1860 made no difference to this problem, 14 years later a Newcastle detective caught a man doing the same thing.

> At the Newcastle Police Court on Monday (28th) a man was charged with having thrown over the wall at the Newcastle Gaol and into the female parade ground, a parcel containing tobacco and cooked meat. The prisoner was seen to commit the offence by Detective Smith who took him into custody. He was fined 40s 0d., and costs.
>
> *Newcastle Courant, Friday August 1st, 1873*

The penalty was modest compared to William Bell's punishment. This easy transfer of things into the prison continued almost until it closed. Children going to school at the Clergy Jubilee School behind the prison would see strings or strong cotton hanging over the prison wall. There would be a match box or similar container on the end containing a few coppers and note asking the finder to buy tobacco or perhaps food and tie it to the end of the string. Then it would hauled back into the prison. With such poor security it was unsurprising that the prison had a limited life.

The Prison Commissioners took over all of the prisons in the United Kingdom in 1877. A few years later they closed Morpeth and Berwick Gaols and sent the prisoners to Newcastle. The Commissioners were also determined to close the Newcastle Gaol at a convenient time on the grounds of its age, insecurity, the inability to extend and develop the prison within its own grounds and also the tight restriction of a town centre site. HM Prison, Newcastle upon Tyne was closed on 31st March 1925.

Persons afflicted

The disease marks on the people in this collection are one of the indicators of the hard lives they led. Their living conditions and the severe over-crowding they experienced in the old, poor-quality houses of 19th century Newcastle upon Tyne, (and in the town's prisons and institutions) left them vulnerable to infectious diseases; cholera, smallpox and typhus are three prime examples. Modern readers may be shocked by the number of offenders in the collection who are recorded as marked by smallpox and having scarred faces. Twenty-one of 67 females across the age range 11 years to 60 were recorded as marked in this way and 31 of 167 males in an age range of 12 to 64 years.

John Bryan is noted as scarred by smallpox.

Descriptions of overcrowded dwellings crop up at regular intervals in this research. In 1867 an investigation reported that 23,000 rooms in Newcastle town centre were the homes for 53,000 people, about half the population of the town.

Henry Armstrong, the Medical Officer of Health for Newcastle, writing in the context of the causes of mortality in the town, stressed the impact of over-crowding and the practices of certain classes.

… That much of the sickness and death in the Borough is due to the Irish portion of the lower classes already referred to there can be little doubt. The general tendency of the Irish to take in lodgers and to overcrowd their too-often dirty dwellings is a matter of common observation, and has been strongly commented on by Dr Russell, the Medical Officer of Health for Glasgow. To this evil Newcastle is probably more exposed than can be surmised from her comparatively large number of immigrants, since those represent but a small part of the Irish in the town.

… Allusion has been made to the love of room-overcrowding among the Irish. This sanitary vice, is however unfortunately not confined to one nationality, nor is its occurrence under the now existing regulations preventable. The Borough requirement of 300 cubic feet of room space per person, though equal to that of many towns, is insufficient for the conservation of health and thoroughly inadequate to the demands of sickness, especially sickness of an infectious kind.

(Report of the Medical Officer of Health on the Sanitary Condition of Newcastle upon Tyne, (for the year 1874) Henry E. Armstrong MRCS)

He also pointed to the prevalence of drunkenness in Newcastle as a 'cause of much sickness and death' in the town. In the year 1874 2,382 men and 876 women were convicted of drunkenness and almost 400 people were treated at the Infirmary for drink-related accidents. He also commented on a curious practice that contributed to the spread of infectious disease.

… Among the causes of disease I have reason to know that the spread of infection is frequently assisted by the bad arrangements connected with the burial of those who have died from fever &c. It is a practice among many undertakers to forbid the opening of the windows of the room where an uncoffined body lies, even though the case has been one of a contagious kind. The crowding together of relatives and neighbours in such places is sometimes great, and the certainty of one or another catching or conveying the contagion is almost inevitable.

Vaccination against smallpox had been developed at the turn of the 18th century by Edward Jenner, who had observed that milkmaids falling ill with cowpox did not later succumb to smallpox. Vaccination of children was made compulsory in 1853. But there is clear evidence in this collection that late into the 19th century certain classes of people would not or could not take advantage of this prevention measure.

On 3rd May 1871 the Mayor of Newcastle upon Tyne issued a public health warning from the Sanitary Committee. 'Having received information that persons afflicted with smallpox have exposed themselves in the streets and other public places', the committee set a fine of up to five pounds for anyone suffering from an infectious disorder and going out in public, any-

Long Stairs, around 1880. People living in conditions like this were poorly nour-
ished, inadequately sheltered and overcrowded. Naturally illness was rife, and mor-
tality was high.

one accompanying them or anyone selling, lending or airing any undisinfected bedding, clothing, rags or other things which had been in contact with sufferers. exposed to infection from such disorders, shall be liable to a penalty not exceeding five pounds. People who let houses or rooms previously occupied by a smallpox sufferer without having them 'disinfected to the satisfaction of a qualified medical practitioner, as testified by a certificate given by him', could be fined up to £20.

This is another clear indicator that not everyone in the town was taking advantage of vaccination, nor taking care not to infect other people. There were several epidemics in the 18th and 19th centuries. In 1882 a Smallpox Hospital was opened on the Town Moor to provide isolation and treatment facilities; the buildings survived into the second half of the 20th century.

About half of the men and women listed in this collection are recorded as having identifying marks of one kind or another, smallpox, other scars, deformities, etc, and the shoeblack burglar Patrick O'Neill, in the first chapter, was even recorded as having webbed feet. A surprise feature is the small number of prisoners with tattoos, just two women and ten men. In the 20th century it was commonplace to find men and women, who had been in prisons and other institutions, to have one or more tattoos, often self-inflicted crude shapes. One of the two women was a 27-year-old married prostitute, born at Shotley Bridge, named Mary Costello alias Quinn.

It is not possible to see any of Costello's tattoos on her photograph, but they are listed as:

Right Breast – Anthony
Right Arm – Anchor, Heart, M.A.C.22, J.M. John McKie, R.Q.S.M.
S.M. E.H.X Anthony McLean
Left Arm – Ellen Watson,
Left Breast – Dixon

Costello had a long run of convictions beginning at 16 in 1861, when she received seven days hard labour as a rogue and vagabond. At 18 years of age, in 1863, she was sentenced to 14 days hard labour for vagrancy. Then followed regular appearances at court for stealing money from the person (probably as a prostitute), taking her to the Newcastle Gaol for six months hard labour at a time. Her latest conviction on 24th February 1872, took her before a High Court Judge, Sir Robert Lush, at the Newcastle Assizes. The

PARTICULARS of a Person convicted of a Crime specified in the 20th Section of the Prevention of Crimes Act, 1871.

Name and aliases } *Mary Costella Quin*

PHOTOGRAPH OF PRISONER.

Description when liberated.

Age (on discharge)......... *27*

Height................... *5.1¾*

Hair...................... *Black*

Eyes..................... *Brown*

Complexion............... *Dark*

Where born.............. *Shotley Bridge*

Married or single.......... *Married*

Trade or occupation........ *Prostitute*

Any other distinguishing mark.................. *Right Breast, Anthony. Right Arm, Anchor, Heart, M. A.E 22. J.M. John McKie R.G. S.M.S.M. E.H.H. Anthony, McLean, Left Arm, Ellen Watson. Left Breast, Dixon*

Part of Mary Costello's form.

combination of yet another charge of stealing money from the person and the long list of previous convictions put her back in the Newcastle Gaol but this time for 15 months hard labour.

James Loxley is as good an example as any of the tattooed male prison-

---

THE SPRING ASSIZES (Tuesday 27th February 1872)
Before Sir Robert Lush

Mary COSTELLO alias Quinn, 26, married, pleaded guilty to an indictment charging her with having on 6th January last stolen from the person of John Roscamp a purse and £8 1s 6d and was sentenced to 15 months imprisonment with hard labour.

Newcastle Courant, Friday March 1st, 1872

ers, with tattoos listed as follows:

Left arm – CI

Back of left hand – J.J.P.O thistle, anchor, ring on each finger

Right hand – ring on 1st and 2nd fingers

Loxley was a stoker, a single man 22 years of age, born at Newcastle.

Description when liberated.	Name and aliases }	James Loxley Oxley	PHOTOGRAPH OF PRISONER.
	Age (on discharge).........	22	
	Height.....................	5.7½	
	Hair....	Brown	
	Eyes..........................	Blue	
	Complexion......	Sallow	
	Where born.................	Newcastle-on-Tyne	
	Married or single...........	Single	
	Trade or occupation........	Striker	
	Any other distinguishing mark..................}	C.I. on left arm, J.J.P.O. thistle anchor on back of left hand, ring on each finger of left hand ring on 1st & 2nd finger of right hand, several scars on both legs.	

ASSAULT AND ROBBERY IN NEWCASTLE

At the Newcastle Police Court yesterday Robert Cruddace and James Loxley, well known to the police, were charged with assaulting and robbing a man named James Lipram in an entry out of the Head of the Side, about eight o'clock on Saturday night. Detective Officers Fawcett and Martin were passing the place when they heard a struggle, and thinking a fight was going on, they went into the passage and found the prisoners ill-using the prosecutor, whose trousers they had torn. Cruddace made his escape out of the passage but was followed by Martin, who captured him after a short chase. Fawcett apprehended Loxley on the spot. The magistrates sent the prisoners to gaol for six months.

Newcastle Daily Chronicle, Tuesday January 14th, 1873

He had no less than 14 previous convictions and prison sentences stretching back to 1863, when he was 12 years of age.

The accomplice, Robert Cruddace, was a 25-year-old labourer, born at

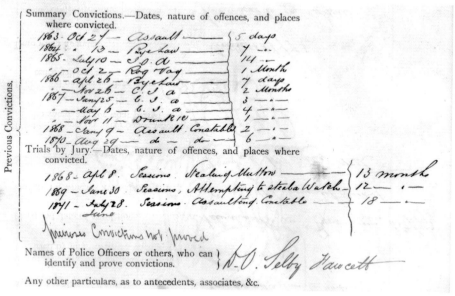

Barnard Castle, with five previous court appearances starting in 1866.

Several photographs in the collection show disabilities of offenders, sometimes quite young people. The photograph of John Reed (see page 98), for example, shows the twisted finger on his left hand; this boy of 15 was already involved in violent thefts on the street. The prison form for Charles Burns (see page 126) is endorsed 'Point of first finger right hand' and the damage can be seen in his photograph.

Thomas Watson, a rough looking character, was sent to the Newcastle Gaol for two months hard labour in May 1873 for stealing a pair of boots. He had lost a finger end at some time in his life, however this not clearly visible in his photograph.

Two other prisoners are noted with similar problems that cannot be seen on their photographs, Isaac Robson, whose right ring finger was deformed, and Thomas Wardman, who had

Thomas Watson.

a finger end amputated.

Several prisoners are recorded as having eye problems, squints and loss of sight. The disfigurement of the left eye of John Kennady is evident in his photograph.

Kennady was a 20-year-old hawker, sent to prison for three months on 9th December 1873 for stealing baskets. His prison form is endorsed 'Cut mark left side of forehead, left eye disfigured.' This young man seemed to be making a career of stealing baskets; he had a previous conviction in 1872 for the same offence.

John Kennady.

In a similar fashion, the form for William Harrison, pictured on page 128, is endorsed 'Left eye blind, wart left cheek, mole on back of right shoulder.'

Lack of sight in one eye did not halt the criminal intentions of Robert Ramshaw, a 35-year-old cart man born at Liverpool.

Ramshaw managed to force his way into the warehouse of George

THE SPRING ASSIZES (Tuesday 27th February 1872)

Before Sir Robert Lush

Robert RAMSHAW, 35 cartman, was indicted for having feloniously on 2nd Day of February last broke and entered a warehouse of George Hudson, cheese and bacon factor, Cloth Market, Newcastle and stealing therein six hams. Mr Green prosecuted and Mr Blackwell defended. Fifteen months imprisonment.

Newcastle Courant, Friday March 1st, 1872

Hudson in the Cloth Market, Newcastle and make off with six hams. This brought Ramshaw before a High Court Judge at the Newcastle Assizes on Tuesday 27th February 1872. Ramshaw received 15 months hard labour for his trouble. This was one of the longer sentences in the records in this collection.

Robert Ramshaw.

Ramshaw had five minor convictions between 1853 and 1864, with short sentences for vagrancy, assault and damage, then nothing until 1873. Where had he been in that time? In prison elsewhere? Back in Liverpool? The prison form for Ramshaw is marked 'Scar and blue mark on nose, left eye blind, 4th finger right hand crooked, several small scars on forehead.'

There are also notes of damaged limbs, twisted noses and other problems scattered throughout this collection of prison forms, all underlining the difficult lives of these men and women. The marks etc. were caused by overcrowding, drunkenness, lack of proper hygiene, life in institutions of one kind or another, lack of medical care (or perhaps unwillingness to seek help) and a lifestyle where violence was a commonly accepted way of resolving problems. Violent crime was sometimes seen as a desperate, but occasionally tempting, way of making a living.

The general appearance of these men and women conforms to a similar pattern. The men as a rule have short hair, not well groomed, probably from self-administered haircuts. For the most part the men are clean shaven, though there are a couple of heavy beards. The common feature for the men and boys is a neckerchief, perhaps wrapped round a couple of times then tied with a knot or bow at the front. Usually a waistcoat is worn over an undershirt, topped by a coat of coarse cloth, often loose and ill fitting.

Anthony Forster is a typical example of a male prisoner. He was a 22-

year-old striker born at Newcastle upon Tyne who was serving six months hard labour for stealing a pair of trousers.

James Augustus Jobling is the only known middle-class prisoner; his photograph and story are at page 20. He appears reasonably smart in a cravat, wing collar, tailored waistcoat and a coat with velvet-covered upper lapels. He is sporting a moustache, wispy mutton chop whiskers and short hair.

The women invariably had their hair tied back and flat to the head. They are pictured wearing a full length dress of a smooth or coarse material in a variety of patterns. Some women wear an apron; others have shoulder capes. Margaret McCann (see page 12) can be seen wearing both. Mary Ann Wiggins was dressed the same way.

In February 1873, Wiggins, a 26-year-old married prostitute, was serving one month hard labour for stealing money from the person. She had four previous commitments to prison; two for stealing money and two minor convictions.

Two male prisoners appear quite different to all the others; they are both wearing military uniform. John Park, a 19-year-old

Anthony Forster.

Mary Ann Wiggins.

man born in Scotland, is described on his prison form as a 'Cartman and soldier, 14th Brigade R.A.' (Royal Artillery). He had no criminal history and there was no newspaper report about his court appearance. A note on the form shows he was convicted of stealing a violin.

The other military man, also with no previous record, was John Thomas. He was described on his form as plasterer and soldier. No regiment is given; his uniform is similar to John Park's but with a brighter braid on the sleeves.

This young man, 20 years of age, was given six months hard labour at the Newcastle Police Court on 23rd January 1873 for stealing a pair of slippers.

John Park.

John Thomas.

'Thank you my lord'

There were just three cases of false pretenses found in this collection of prison records. The first was Charles Burns. He was a 19-year-old miner, born in Liverpool, with no record of convictions, and quite smartly dressed in his photograph compared with many of the others.

Burns appeared before the Recorder at the Newcastle Quarter Sessions at the Guildhall in April 1873 and was given three months hard labour at the Newcastle Gaol for obtaining or endeavouring to obtain (depending upon which newspaper report is correct) a pair of trousers and a waistcoat by false pretenses. The lack of detail is frustrating but it appears he may have falsely represented himself to be someone else to obtain the clothing.

Charles Burns.

NEWCASTLE SESSIONS

Saturday 12th April 1873 before Mr J.P. Mulgrave, Deputy Recorder

Charles Burns, 19 years, miner, pleaded guilty to obtaining from Daniel M'Killop by false pretenses, a pair of trousers, a coat and a waistcoat, the property of John Milling. The prosecutor William Harrison, in whose name the prisoner obtained the goods, did not press the charge, sentenced to three months imprisonment.

Newcastle Daily Chronicle, Monday April 14th, 1873

(At the Newcastle Quarter Sessions before the Deputy Recorder Mr J.P. Mulcaster)

Charles Burns (19), miner, pleaded guilty to a charge of attempting and endeavouring to obtain from one Daniel McKillop, a pair of trousers and a waistcoat, with intent to defraud one John Mulling, on 5th April 1873. He was sentenced to three months imprisonment.

Newcastle Courant, Friday April 18th, 1873

The Guildhall, where Charles Burn was tried at the Quarter Sessions. This photograph was taken around 1893.

There is equally sparse information about the second case. William Harrison was a labourer born at Durham. By some sort of trick or false pretence, he managed to obtain five and a half stone of oats (77 pounds). He would have needed a barrow to transport them! According to press reports, Harrison worked his false pretence on Sarah Renwick who most probably was a servant of the actual owners of the oats.

William Harrison.

THE SPRING ASSIZES (Tuesday 27th February 1872)
Before Sir Robert Lush

William Harrison, 51, labourer, was indicted for having on the 15th October last, unlawfully and knowingly obtained by certain false pretenses of Sarah Renwick, 5¹/₂ stone of oats, the property of Sarah Marion Hume and another with intent to defraud them of the same. Mr Edge prosecuted; the prisoner was undefended, twelve months imprisonment with hard labour.

Newcastle Courant, Friday March 1st, 1872

Given the distinctive appearance of Harrison, obtaining goods by false pretenses was a seriously risky business. Yet his previous conviction list includes six months hard labour at Newcastle Quarter Sessions in 1866 and nine months hard labour at the Newcastle Assizes in 1869 both convictions for obtaining oats by false pretenses.

The third case, involved three confidence tricksters relieving a pitman from Haswell Colliery of money and a watch by 'Thimble Rigging', a variation on the old gambling fraud, the three card trick. The skilled leader of the gang rapidly moves around three thimbles and the 'mark' or victim is drawn into betting on which thimble has the pea under it. Of course the victim has no fair chance of winning. The gang consisted of James Davit, Thomas Smith alias Woodhall, and a man named William Cotter. Although all three were found guilty, the Recorder then advised the jury that certain features about Cotter's actions meant he should have been found not guilty so Cotter was duly acquitted.

James Davit was an 18-year-old single man born in Ireland, with no previous convictions recorded on his form. His first accomplice, who took a leading role in this affair, was Thomas Smith alias Woodhall, a 32-year-old shoemaker born in New York, USA. This heavily bearded figure was recorded as a widower. Smith had two previous convictions, both for stealing coats; in 1861, two months hard labour, and in 1862 when he was sent to prison for six months hard labour. It appears he stayed out of trouble for ten years until 23rd November 1872, when he struck up a conversation with Charles Penman at the Central Railway Station and persuaded the man to join him for a drink at a bar in the town. Why Penman agreed to interrupt a journey to Carlisle to have a drink with a stranger is not at all clear.

James Davitt and Thomas Smith, confidence tricksters.

His new friend took him to a bar off the Bigg Market, where there just happened to be two friends of Smith playing a game with thimbles and a pea. Penman innocently watched the game and of course was eventually drawn to make wagers. The game was a complete sham and he lost money and his watch. However, the gullible Mr Penman, realising he had been duped, went off and found a constable and the gang were arrested. At the time of the 1881 census, Charles Penman, a 30-year-old colliery banksman, was living at Fifth Cross Road, Haswell Colliery with his wife and two daughters. The Tyneside press were very interested in this unusual case.

THIMBLE RIGGING

William Cotter (42) hawker, James Davit (19) hawker, and Thomas Smith alias Woodhall, shoemaker, were charged with cheating and defrauding one Charles Penman of the sum of £2 and a watch on 21st November. Mr Stevenson prosecuted; and Mr Blackwell defended Cotter. The prosecutor who belonged to Haswell Colliery met the prisoner Smith at the Central Station on the morning of 21st November. The latter asked him to have a walk in the town. They went to the Crown and Thistle back bar where they were soon joined by the prisoners Cotter and Davit. The prisoners produced some thimbles and peas and commenced the 'thimble rigging' game, prosecutor watched them playing for money and exchanging coin. He was at length urged by the prisoner Smith to make a bet which thimble the pea was in, at first he refused but at length made a bet of £2 and lost. He also staked his watch against Smith's and again lost. Prosecutor then left the house and gave information to the police. The prisoners were then found guilty by the jury; but the learned Recorder said there were certain features in Cotter's case which made him different from the other prisoners, and he would have been better satisfied if the jury had acquitted him. However as the sentence had not been recorded, he would allow the jury, if they wished, to reconsider their verdict. The jury after a brief consultation gave him the benefit of the doubt. Davit was sentenced to six weeks imprisonment. Smith against whom there were previous convictions was committed for three months.

Newcastle Daily Journal, Thursday 2nd January 1873

Pubs in the Bigg Market, near Pudding Chare, 1880.

The journalist of the *Newcastle Daily Chronicle* reported an amusing conclusion to the case caused by Davit's reaction to his sentence being shorter than that for Smith.

The prosecutor who belonged to Haswell, was in the Central Station on the morning of the day named in the indictment, when Smith went up to him and asked him where he was going. He said he was going to Carlisle, and Smith then asked him to go and have a glass … at the back bar of the Crown and Thistle, Pudding Chare.

After sentence Davit said to the Recorder, 'Thank you, my Lord, I didn't expect to get off so safe.' (Laughter)

The Newcastle Daily Chronicle, Thursday January 2nd, 1873

Gaol for young and old

Very little information has survived in the newspapers and other archives about young prisoners in the collection. The youngest was a girl called Ellen Woodman, 11 years of age and born in Durham. In the 1881 census, Ellen Woodman, now 18, and designated as a housekeeper, was recorded as living at 72 Thames Street, Westoe as daughter of Robert Bold and Catherine Bold. The reason for a different surname in the family unit is not apparent; presumably her mother Catherine had married again.

Ellen Woodman, aged 11.

Ellen appeared before the Newcastle magistrates on Tuesday 2nd May 1873 with three other young girls. Mary Catherine Docherty aged 14 and born in Newcastle, Mary Hinnigan aged 13 and also born at Newcastle and Rosanna Watson aged 13, born in Durham. They were jointly charged with stealing iron, probably scrap metal. None of these four girls had any history of previous convictions, but nevertheless, the magistrates sent each one of them to seven days hard labour in the Newcastle Gaol.

This punishment, extraordinary to modern eyes, passed unreported in the Tyneside newspapers.

Mary Catherine Docherty, age 14.

Mary Hinnigan, age 13.

The faces of these four young girls are among the most poignant in the collection. What sort of lives did they lead after their seven days of hard labour? They are understandably distressed, their clothes are unkempt, and Ellen Woodman, the youngest, looks malnourished.

Rosanna Watson, age 13.

The oldest offender in this collection was John Roman.

According to his prison form he was a tailor, 64 years of age, married and had been born in Germany. Roman, a man with no recorded criminal history, appeared before the Newcastle magistrates at the Manors Police Court on 24th February 1873, charged with stealing clothing belonging to a man named John Jacobs. The background circumstances are unknown as the case was not reported in the press. Whatever they were, this elderly man with long mutton-chop whiskers was sent to the Newcastle Gaol for 14 days and put to hard labour.

John Roman.

Champagne and low haunts

O ne of the most famous inns in Newcastle, with a history going back many centuries, is the Old Queen's Head in Pilgrim Street. The building, advertised below in 1855, has been renovated in recent years and is now known as Alderman Fenwick's house.

BURGLARIES IN NEWCASTLE

David Barron, 19 years of age was charged with breaking and entering into the Old Queen's Head Inn, Pilgrim Street, and stealing therefrom seven bottles of champagne, a quantity of rum, and three shillings in copper at an early hour on Thursday morning. A young man named Thomas Sanderson said he was in William Hill's workshop where he heard the prisoner and Hill concocting a plan to open one of the doors of the inn with a key, and sometime after they came into the workshop with seven bottles of champagne and some rum. They did not say where they got them, but said they forced the side door to the front bar. Part of the champagne was drunk in the workshop between one and two o'clock in the morning. The prisoner pleaded guilty to the charge and was sent to gaol for six months.

Newcastle Daily Chronicle, Saturday August 24th, 1872

David Barron was a 19-year old cabinet maker, born at Newcastle upon Tyne. William Hill, a 28-year-old cabinet maker who had a workshop in the Old Queen's Head Yard was probably his employer. Barron had no previous convictions but William Hill, who was described in other newspaper reports as a 'well known character,' had five convictions including warehousebreaking and had been out of prison for just 24 hours before he began scheming with Barron. Hill evaded capture for about a week then went back to gaol for six months hard labour.

David Barron.

BURGLARY AT NEWCASTLE

At the Newcastle Police Court yesterday before Aldermen Pollard and Wilson:-

William Hill, 28 years of age, pleaded guilty to breaking and entering the Old Queen's Head public-house, Pilgrim Street, early on the morning of the 22nd August, in company with another person and stealing therefrom seven bottles of champagne, a quantity of spirits and three shillings in copper. The prisoner's companion, who was captured shortly after the robbery, on the following day, was sentenced to be imprisoned for six months. The magistrates sent the prisoner to gaol for the same period.

Newcastle Daily Chronicle, Friday August 30th, 1872

William Hill.

Pickpockets and prostitutes were not the only groups of people troubling pedestrians on the streets of Victorian Newcastle. In January 1873 a Newcastle citizen wrote a long-winded letter to the *Journal* on the subject of beggars.

Letter of complaint: STREET BEGGARS IN NEWCASTLE

[long letter referring to Grey Street, Grainger Street and elsewhere]

'**How is it that Newcastle is infected to such an extent as it is with street beggars ... one of whom seems to be permanently stationed in that locality** [Grainger Street]? **This gentleman sitting squat upon a heap of dirty straw in the muddiest part of the street with his head enveloped in a filthy rag, represents a very elaborate as well as repulsive picture of misery.**'

[then the writer goes on to complain that the beggars ...]

'**... retire to their low haunts**' [and spend their alms] '**in drunken revelry with the vilest of thieves.**'

Newcastle Daily Journal, Wednesday January 8th, 1873

The east side of Sandhill, towards the Quayside, around 1865-70. Most of these houses would be replaced by new office buildings from the 1880s. The shop with the projecting front belonged to W.B. Proctor, lamp merchant and canvas manufacturer. He also dealt in guano (fertiliser made from bird droppings).

Sandhill, looking north, around 1880. The camera was a source of fascination for these little boys. The Guildhall is on the left.

An organ grinder on Grey Street in 1895.

On the left is the Central Exchange where Thomas Charles Grainger received a note from James Augustus Jobling before he was assaulted by him in November 1872.

Newgate Street, 1881. There was a garotte robbery on this street in 1871 for which the culprit, John Smith, was flogged with the cat o' nine tails and sent to prison for four years (see page 112).

Appendix 1: the Collection

On the following pages is a complete schedule of all the persons named in the collection, sorted alphabetically by surname, plus a number of personal details.

The headings for the columns from left to right are as follows:

T&W = The Tyne and Wear Archives number for each individual

SURNAME = Surname

FORENAME = Forenames

SEX = M = male F = female

AGE = Age on the day of discharge from prison.

S/M/W = single, married or widow(er)

POB = Place of birth as recorded on the prison form

OCCUP = Occupation as recorded on the prison form

CON DATE = Date of conviction

OFFENCE/SENTENCE = Offence and prison sentence

'Theft money p' means stealing money from the person of another, such as picking pockets, stealing purses etc.

'3 c/mths HL' and similar, mean sentenced to three calendar months imprisonment with hard labour.

'10 day HL + 5 yrs RS', this and similar sentences refer to young persons and mean sentenced to ten days hard labour in prison (sometimes with the first and last day in solitary confinement) followed by five years in a reformatory school.

OFFICER = Name of the Newcastle Police Officer or North Eastern Railway Police Office (NER) who can identify the prisoner.

T&W	Surname	Forename	Sex	Age	s/m/w	POB	Occup	Con date	Offence/sentence	Officer
1277	ALLAN	John	M	19	S	Wark	Labourer	1873/02/06	Theft money p, 6 c/mths HL	PC J.White
1201	ALLAN	Edward	M	20	S	Kent	Boilermkr	1873/02/24	Theft cap, 3 c/mths HL	PC 25.Lowry
1218	ALLAN	Effie	F	22	S	Gateshead	Prostitute	1872/12/05	Theft money p, 6 c/mths HL	PC 34 T.Hunter
1258	ANDERSON	James	M	18	S	Scotland	Labourer	1873/03/18	Theft clothes, 4 c/mths HL	PC 11 Rutherford
1262	ARMSTRONG	Agnes Ann	F	23	M	Berwick	None	1873/01/17	Theft money p, 6 c/mths HL	PC 14 M.Smith
1289	ARMSTRONG	Elizabeth	F	36	M	Newcastle	Charw'n	1873/05/19	Theft mat, 3 c/mths HL	DO Smith
1133	BADGER	William	M	20	S	Newcastle	Shoem'ker	1872/09/12	Theft watch, 6 c/mths HL	PC 31 B.Percy
1295	BAKER	John	M	18	S	Gateshead	Labourer	1873/07/28	Theft poultry, 7 days HL	PC20 J.Relfe
1112	BARCLAY	Thomas	M	22	S	Berwick	Groom	1872/11/01	Theft money p, 4 c/mths HL	Sgt. R.Anderson
1099	BARRON	David	M	19	S	Newcastle	Cabt mkr	1872/08/23	Theft champagne, 6 c/mths HL.	DO Thorburn
1266	BAXTER	Margaret	F	42	M	Dundee	None	1873/06/30	Theft beef, 14 days HL	PC 29 Grey
1134	BELL	Thomas	M	17	S	Newcastle	Striker	1872/09/13	Theft watch, 6 c/mths HL	DO G.Anderson
1137	BELL	George	M	24	S	Hexham	Striker	1873/01/31	Theft watches, 2 c/mths HL	DO G. Anderson
1219	BELL	James	M	27	M	Scotland	Draper	1872/12/09	Theft coat, 6 c/mths HL	PC M.Thorburn
1131	BELL	William	M	32	M	Newcastle	Bl/smith	1872/09/16	Theft beef, 6 c/mths HL	PC 33 J.Tilley
1146	BENNETT	Elizabeth	F	28	M	Darlington	Needlew'n	1873/02/06	Theft money p, 2 c/mths HL	PC Tough, NER
1106	BOGAN	Edward	M	24	S	Newcastle	Glassmkr	1872/11/25	Theft tea, 3 c/mths HL	PC 20 J.Relfe
1114	BOLAM	Robert	M	20	S	Gateshead	Labourer	1872/09/03	Theft clothes, 6 c/mths HL	DO S.Fawcett
1257	BOLTON	Robert	M	17	S	Newcastle	Bootcloser	1873/04/17	Theft watch, 3 c/mths HL	DO A.Martin
1300	BOLTON	John	M	26	S	Newcastle	Shoemker	1873/02/27	Theft leather, 6 c/mths HL	DO A.Martin
1143	BONE	James	M	19	S	Sth Shields	Mason	1873/01/07	Theft ham, 3 c/mths HL	PC 5 Rbt.Bell
1171	BRADSHAW	Richard	M	40	M	Ireland	Hawker	1872/10/31	Theft money p, 6 c/mth HL	DO A.Martin
1196	BRADY	Bridget	F	18	S	Felling	Servant	1873/04/28	Theft gold pen, 14 days HL	Sgt. J.Armstrong
1181	BRANKSTON	William	M	43	M	Alnwick	Labourer	1873/04/08	Theft rabbits, 1 c/mth HL	DO Davison NER
1197	BREWIS	Mary	F	19	S	Newcastle	Servant	1873/01/23	Theft clothes, 4 c/mths HL	A/Sgt Martin
1241	BROOMFIELD	Joseph	M	33	W	Newcastle	Painter	1873/01/06	Theft money p, 6 c/mths HL	PC 15 W.King

T&W	Surname	Forename	Sex	Age	s/m/w	POB	Occup	Con date	Offence/sentence	Officer
1104	BROWN	Ellen or Jane	F	25	M	Berrycop?	Prostitute	1872/10/29	Theft money p. 4 c/mths HL	PC 29 J.Grey
1264	BROWN	Mary Jane	F	36	W	Cumberl'd	Charw'n	1873/01/24	Theft chairs, 6 c/mths HL	PC 25 R.Todd
1215	BROWN	George	M	42	M	Burslow	Labourer	1873/04/29	Theft money p, 1 c/mth HL	PC 10 Graves
1226	BRYAN	John	M	29	S	Newcastle	Waterman	1873/02/20	Theft lead, 4 c/mths HL	Insp Moffatt
1238	BURDIS	Thomas	M	42	S	Bywell	Labourer	1873/01/02	Theft cart cover, 6 c/mths HL	DO S.Fawcett
1225	BURNS	Ann	F	18	S	Newcastle	Prostitute	1873/05/20	Theft waistcoat, 1 c/mth HL	PC28 Rutherford
1253	BURNS	Charles	M	19	S	Liverpool	Miner	1873/04/12	False pretenses, 3 c/mths HL	Supt Scott
1244	CAIN	Catherine	F	23	S	Liverpool	Prostitute	1873/04/07	Theft money p 3 c/mths HL	PC 39 T.Bigg
1124	CALDER	Joseph	M	19	S	Edinburgh	Labourer	1873/01/26	Theft plane, 6 c/mths HL	DO M.Thorburn
1302	CALDER	Joseph	M	19	S	Edinburgh	Labourer	1873/04/28	Theft blanket, 4 c/mths HL	Sgt. Johnston
1159	CALDER	James	M	29	M	Scotland	Butcher	1873/03/27	Theft pail, 14 days HL	Sgt R.Anderson
1142	CAMPBELL	Alexander	M	56	M	Scotland	Joiner	1872/10/04	Theft clothes, 6 c/mths HL	PC 28 J.Hall
1230	CARLISLE	Jane	F	29	M	Cumb'land	Hawker	1873/04/17	Theft bed linen, 2 c/mths HL	DO S.Fawcett
1228	CARR	Ann	F	36	S	Newcastle	Fact'y Hnd	1873/02/21	Theft money p, 4 c/mths HL	PC 16 Archbold
1234	CARTNER	Jane	F	22	M	Newcastle	Prostitute	1872/12/26	Theft watch p, 6 c/mths HL	DO Smith
1082	CASSIDY	Sarah	F	24	S	Newcastle	Prostitute	1872/11/29	Theft money p, 2 c/mths HL	DO Martin
1139	CASSIDY	Margaret	F	25	M	Bradford	None	1873/01/31	Theft money p, 2 c/mths HL	PC A.Percy
1128	CHARLTON	Robert	M	16	S	Newcastle	Labourer	1872/11/11	Theft boots, 4 c/mths HL	Insp. M.Hepple
1161	CHRISTIE	Mary Erskine	F	32	M	Gateshead	Prostitute	1872/10/22	Theft money p, 6 c/mths HL	DO Martin
1204	CLARK	John	M	19	S	Newcastle	Joiner	1873/02/20	Theft plane, 3 c/mths HL	PC. S.Fawcett
1121	CLEMENTSON	Thomas	M	17	S	Newcastle	Striker	1873/01/26	Theft plane 6 wks HL	DO M.Thorburn
1248	CLUSKY	Peter	M	20	S	Newcastle	Labourer	1873/05/12	Theft pork, 2 c/mths HL	DO J.Smith
1169	CONNOLLY	Bernard	M	23	S	Ch Le St	Labourer	1873/01/30	Theft money p, 3 c/mths HL	DO S.Fawcett
1207	CONNOR	Daniel	M	28	S	Newcastle	Tinsmith	1873/04/29	Theft money, 14 days HL	Sgt. Johnston
1103	COSH	Margaret	F	15	S	Newcastle	None	1872/12/26	Theft coat, 2 c/mths HL	A/Sgt. Henderson
1198	COSTELLO	Mary	F	27	M	Sh Bridge	Prostitute	1873/02/24	Theft money p, 15 c/mths HL	PC Davison NER

T&W	Surname	Forename	Sex	Age	s/m/w	POB	Occup	Con date	Offence/sentence	Officer
1239	COULSON	James	M	22	S	Newcastle	Bootsetter	1872/07/03	Theft watches, 12 c/mths HL	PC P.Turnbull
1222	COYLE	Clement	M	13	S	Aldershot	Errand boy	1873/05/22	Theft clothes, 14 d HL + 5 yrs	PC 15 Wood
1185	COYLE	Ellen	F	19	S	Nth Shlds	Prostitute	1873/02/14	Theft clothes, 3 c/mths HL	Sgt. James
1252	CRUDDACE	Robert	M	25	S	Bd Castle	Labourer	1873/01/13	Theft money p. 6 c/mths HL	DO Martin
1160	CRUMBIE	Mary Ann	F	30	M	Glasgow	None	1873/03/27	Att. Theft money, 7 days HL	PC 4 J.Potts
1237	CURRY	John	M	18	S	Newcastle	Waterman	1873/04/01	Theft money, 3 c/mths HL	DO G.Anderson
1092	DAKIN	Henry	M	22	S	London	Labourer	1873/01/20	Theft chisels, 14 days HL	PC J.K.Archbold
1125	DARLEY	James	M	16	S	Shotley Br	Labourer	1873/01/09	Theft shirts, 2 c/mths HL	PC 34 T.Hunter
1212	DAVISON	Harriet	F	39	W	Hull	Laundress	1873/03/27	Theft money p. 2 c/mths HL	PC J.Smith
1097	DAVIT	James	M	18	S	Ireland	Hawker	1873/01/01	Conspiracy, 6 weeks HL	PC J.Forster
1157	DEES	Elizabeth	F	29	M	Newcastle	None	1873/02/21	Theft books, 2 c/mths HL	PC 12 J.Taylor
1179	DENHAM	Thomas	M	27	S	Newcastle	Labourer	1873/04/10	Theft books, 14 days HL	PC 31 A.Percy
1286	DIVINE	John	M	17	S	Ireland	Carver	1873/02/17	Theft money p. 6 c/mths HL	DO Martin
1249	DIXON	Peter	M	19	S	Yorkshire	Labourer	1873/05/12	Theft watch, 2 c/mths HL	Det Supt. Moore
1278	DIXON	Thomas	M	20	S	Newcastle	Fireman	1873/02/06	Theft money p. 6 c/mths HL	PC J.White
1208	DOCHERTY	Mary Catherine	F	14	S	Newcastle	None	1873/05/02	Theft iron, 7 days HL	PC 25 T.Lowrey
1274	DODDS	Isabella	F	17	S	Liverpool	Servant	1873/04/03	Theft watch, 4 c/mths HL	DO G.Anderson
1184	DRYBURGH	Jane	F	40	W	Chester	Charw'n	1873/04/07	Theft eggs, 1 c/mth HL	PC 32 G.Batey
1190	DUFFY	John	M	16	S	Newcastle	Labourer	1872/11/15	Theft money, 6 c/mths HL	PC 11 Rutherford
1191	DUFFY	Peter	M	20	S	Newcastle	Boltmker	1872/11/15	Theft money, 6 c/mths HL	PC 24 A.Stokoe
1298	DUFFY	Michael	M	21	S	Ireland	Labourer	1873/05/26	Theft money p. 3 c/mths HL	PC 24 Hunter
1122	DUNLOP	Robert	M	24	S	Scotland	Joiner	1873/02/10	Theft watch, 1 c/mth HL	Sgt. W.Percy
1297	EADE	Arthur Charles	M	24	S	Uckfield	Clrk	1873/07/31	Theft, 7 days HL	PC 21 Lowtham
1148	EMMERTON	George	M	23	S	Newcastle	Labourer	1873/03/17	Theft clothes, 21 days HL	PC 23 Hammond
1090	FARRELL	Jane	F	12	S	Newcastle	None	1873/01/06	Theft books, 10 day HL, 5 yrs	DO G.Anderson
1176	FENN	Edward	M	15	S	Woolwich	Bobbinwdr	1873/03/31	Theft clothes, 1 c/mth HL	PC 19 Teford

T&W	Surname	Forename	Sex	Age	s/m/w	POB	Occup	Con date	Offence/sentence	Officer
1101	FENNADY	James	M	21	S	Stockport	B'layer	1872/12/24	Theft, 2 c/mths HL	PC 8 A.Wetherall
1172	FISHER	Michael Clement	M	13	S	W H'pool	None	1873/01/01	Housebreaking 4 c/mths HL	DO G.Anderson
1229	FLYNN	Catherine	F	34	M	Ireland	Hawker	1873/03/17	Theft money p, 3 c/mths HL	Sgt R.Anderson
1242	FORBES	Sabina	F	32	M	Newcastle	Prostitute	1873/01/07	Theft money p, 6 c/mths HL	PC 22 A.Guntup
1081	FORSTER	Anthony	M	22	S	Hull	Striker	1872/08/01	Theft trousers, 6 c/mths HL	DO S.Fawcett
1240	FOX	Robert	M	24	S	Newcastle	Fireman	1873/06/05	Theft trousers, 1 c/mth HL	PC 13 J.Casely
1250	FOX	John	M	40	M	Ireland	Labourer	1873/01/13	Receiving, 6 c/mths HL	Det Supt Moore
1089	GARRATY	Patrick	M	15	S	Newcastle	None	1873/01/09	Theft shirts, 1 c/mth HL	PC 34 T.Hunter
1116	GARRATY	Thomas	M	18	S	Gateshead	Labourer	1872/08/29	Theft clothes, 6 c/mths HL	DO S.Fawcett
1265	GARRETT	Ann	F	22	S	Newcastle	Prostitute	1873/06/26	Theft money p, 1 c/mth HL	PC 29 Grey
1301	GIBBONS	John	M	20	S	Newcastle	Labourer	1873/05/27	Theft, 3 c/mths HL	DO S. Fawcett
1119	GIBSON	George	M	23	M	Newcastle	Fitter	1873/01/06	Theft clothes, 2 c/mths HL	DO M.Thorburn
1270	GIBSON	James	M	29	M	Newcastle	Labourer	1873/06/23	Theft money, 1 c/mth HL	PC 34 Stewart
1178	GILBOY	Mary	F	17	S	Morpeth	Servant	1873/04/01	Theft clothes, 1 c/mth HL	PC 24 W.Davison
1095	GORDON	John	M	18	S	Newcastle	Labourer	1873/01/14	Theft boots 1 c/mth HL	PC 16 R.Garget
1280	GORDON	John (younger)	M	18	S	Newcastle	Labourer	1873/05/08	Theft clothes, 3 c/mths HL	PC G.Lisle
1232	GORDON	William	M	23	M	Leeds	Labourer	1873/04/28	Theft money p, 2 c/mths HL	Sgt R.Anderson
1272	GRAHAM	Robert	M	24	S	Newcastle	Tinsmith	1873/06/23	Theft money, 1 c/mth HL	PC 23 A.Guntup
1245	GRAHAM	Maria	F	45	S	Carlisle	Charw'n	1873/04/07	Theft money p 3 c/mths HL	PC 29 T.Bigg
1152	GRANT	Alexander	M	25	S	Glasgow	Sailor	1873/03/18	Theft sheets, 21 days HL	PC 11 Rutherford
1150	GREEN	John	M	21	S	Ireland	Labourer	1873/02/11	Theft books, 2 c/mths HL	PC 29 W. Beattie
1132	GREEN	Samuel	M	23	S	Newcastle	Labourer	1873/02/03	Theft, 6 wks HL	Supt G.Turnel
1193	GREY	Mary Ann	F	23	M	Newcastle	None	1873/04/15	Theft clothes, 14 days HL	DO Martin
1231	GRIEVESON	John	M	21	S	Newcastle	Clerk	1873/02/24	Theft pigeons, 4 c/mths HL	DO G.Anderson
1192	HAIGH	Thomas	M	17	S	Askern,Yk	Sailor	1873/04/18	Theft watch p, 1 c/mth HL	PC Smeaton SSh
1206	HAIR	Frank	M	20	S	Newcastle	Shoemkr	1873/04/24	Theft clothes, 14 days HL	PC 10 R.Graves

T&W	Surname	Forename	Sex	Age	s/m/w	POB	Occup	Con date	Offence/sentence	Officer
1233	HALL	Michael or John	M	38	S	Gateshead	Weaver	1872/12/30	Theft watch etc, 6 c/mths HL	DO Martin
1247	HANAGAN	David	M	43	S	Hanley	Plasterer	1873/06/09	Theft trowel, 1 c/mth HL	PC 33 T.Charlton
1186	HANNAH	Ann	F	37	M	Ireland	Hawker	1873/03/10	Theft oranges, 2 c/mths HL	Sgt A.Patterson
1174	HARDY	Robert	M	21	S	Corbridge	Signalman	1873/01/01	Theft ale, 4 c/mths HL	Insp Craig NER
1098	HARRISON	William	M	51	M	Durham	Porter	1872/02/24	False pretenses 12 c/mths HL	DO S.Fawcett
1296	HARVEY	William	M	36	S	Ireland	Cutler	1873/07/31	Theft, 7 days HL	Sgt. D.James
1259	HEADS	William	M	16	S	Newcastle	Polisher	1873/04/21	Theft money, 3 c/mths HL	PC McEwen
1110	HILL	William	M	28	S	Newcastle	Joiner	1872/08/29	Theft money, 6 c/mths HL	DO M.Thorburn
1223	HILL	Elizabeth	F	54	W	Edinburgh	Charw'n	1873/03/20	Theft sheet, 3 c/mths HL	Sgt R.Anderson
1195	HINDMARSH	Isabella	F	16	S	Gateshead	Servant	1873/04/15	Theft money, 1 c/mth HL	PC 28 M.Hall
1141	HINES	Michael	M	17	S	Leeds	Miner	1872/12/03	Theft umbrellas, 4 c/mths HL	DO G.Anderson
1210	HINNIGAN	Mary	F	13	S	Newcastle	None	1873/05/02	Theft iron, 7 days HL	PC 25 T.Lowrey
1079	HOBSON	John	M	22	S	Newcastle	Labourer	1872/10/28	Theft clothes, 3 c/mths HL	Sgt James Allan
1182	HOPE	William	M	24	S	Newcastle	Cartman	1873/03/10	Theft coal, 2 c/mths HL	DO Martin
1118	HOWARD	Robert	M	23	S	Newcastle	None	1873/02/10	Theft mat, 7 days HL	PC Rutherford
1236	HUNTER	Stephen	M	17	S	Newcastle	Labourer	1873/04/01	Theft money, 3 c/mths HL	DO G.Anderson
1271	IRELAND	William	M	28	M	Newcastle	Labourer	1873/06/23	Theft money p, 1 c/mth HL	PC 33 Charlton
1083	IRVING	Mary Ann	F	37	S	Ireland	Charw'n	1872/11/29	Theft money p, 2 c/mths HL	DO Martin
1085	JEFFREY	Mary	F	38	M	Aberdeen	None	1873/01/10	Theft umbrella, 7 days HL	PC F.Rutherford
1235	JOBEY	Joseph	M	18	S	Newcastle	Miner	1873/04/01	Theft money, 3 c/mths HL	DO G.Anderson
1080	JOBLING	James Augustus	M	26	S	Newcastle	Merchant	1873/01/01	Wounding, 1 c/mth	PC 20 J.Belper
1164	JOBSON	Charles	M	20	M	Leeds	Labourer	1873/03/24	Theft money p, 1 c/mth HL	PC 11 Rutherford
1111	JOHNSON	Robert	M	24	M	Berwick	Dealer	1872/11/01	Theft money p, 4 c/mths HL	PC 33 Charlton
1213	JOHNSON	Mary	F	25	M	Newcastle	Hawker	1873/04/28	Theft money p, 1 c/mth HL	Sgt R.Anderson
1273	JOYCE	Martin	M	22	S	Ireland	Labourer	1873/01/27	Theft clothes, 6 c/mths HL	PC Robson NER
1260	KELLY	Catherine	F	17	S	Nottinghm	Prostitute	1873/04/17	Theft bed linen, 3 c/mths HL	DO S.Fawcett

T&W	Surname	Forename	Sex	Age	s/m/w	POB	Occup	Con date	Offence/sentence	Officer
1120	KENNADY	John	M	20	S	Newcastle	Hawker	1873/12/09	Theft baskets, 3 c/mths HL	DO M.Rathie
1194	KIRK	Ann	F	35	S	Ireland	Charw'n	1873/02/14	Theft money p, 3 c/mths HL	PC 27 J.Foster
1220	LAIDLER	John	M	22	S	Newcastle	Striker	1873/05/15	Theft money, 14 days HL	PC 33 G.Batey
1130	LAMB	George	M	17	S	Newcastle	Cartman	1872/11/15	Theft money p, 4 c/mths HL	PC M.Rutherford
1246	LEE	George	M	39	M	Felling	Traveller	1873/04/08	Theft money, 3 c/mths HL	Sgt. James
1299	LIDDLE	Alexander	M	15	S	Gateshead	Labourer	1873/06/26	Theft money, 2 c/mths HL	Sgt. D.James
1251	LOXLEY	James	M	22	S	Newcastle	Stoker	1873/01/13	Theft money p, 6 c/mths HL	DO S.Fawcett
1086	LUVELLE	John	M	17	S	Gateshead	Miner	1873/01/06	Theft money, 1 c/mth HL	Supt. T.Watson
1293	MALLON	Felix or Hugh	M	28	S	Durham	Labourer	1873/02/24	Theft money, 6 c/mths HL	Insp Pringle
1263	MARTIN	Grace	F	46	M	Newcastle	Hawker	1873/06/19	Theft money p, 1 c/mth HL	PC 32 J.Frazer
1093	MAULS	Robert	M	20	S	Alnwick	Trimmer	1873/11/12	Theft money p, 3 c/mths HL	PC R.Graves
1243	McCANN	Margaret	F	24	S	Newcastle	Hawker	1873/01/07	Theft money p, 6 c/mths HL	PC 22 A.Guntup
1288	McCASFREY	Mary Ann	F	41	M	Newcastle	Hawker	1873/04/18	Theft watch, 4 c/mths HL	DO M.Thorburn
1189	McCONNELL	John	M	22	S	Newcastle	Shingler	1873/04/14	Theft bottles, 1 c/mth HL	PC T.Hunter
1144	McFARLANE	James	M	18	S	Felling Sh.	Glassmkr	1873/03/06	Theft hat, 1 c/mth HL	PC 31 A.Percy
1094	MCKIE	David	M	31	M	Newcastle	Fitter	1873/01/13	Theft cloth, 1 c/mth HL,	PC 29 J.Grey
1126	McKINLEY	Ann	F	31	S	Glasgow	Prostitute	1872/09/09	Theft sugar, 6 c/mths HL	PC 20 J.Relfe
1147	MIDDLETON	Margaret	F	25	S	Manch'ter	Prostitute	1873/03/17	Theft clothes, 14 days HL	PC 11 R.Moffatt
1282	MILLER	Henry	M	14	S	Berwick	Confectnr	1873/07/14	Theft clothes, 14 days HL	DO M.Smith
1100	MILLER	William	M	29	S	Newcastle	Labourer	1872/10/24	Theft oats, 4 c/mths HL	PC 20 J.Relfe
1107	MOFFATT	William	M	17	S	Newcastle	Labourer	1872/12/26	Theft apples, 2 c/mths HL	PC 19 J.Wilkinson
1153	MOFFATT	William	M	28	S	Dumfries	Bricklyr	1873/01/16	Theft money, 3 c/mths HL	PC 29 Richardson
1294	MONAGHAN	Stephen	M	14	S	Scotland	None	1873/07/25	Theft money p, 10 day HL, 3 yrs	PC 21 Gowthain
1217	MORRISON	Eliz Armstrong	F	18	S	Scotland	Servant	1873/03/04	Theft washing, 3 c/mths HL	PC 14 J.Smith
1123	MORRISON	John	M	24	S	Newcastle	Groom	1872/12/09	Theft money p, 3 c/mths HL	PC 31 A.Percy
1096	MORTON	John	M	18	S	Stockton	Labourer	1873/12/16	Theft shawl, 2 c/mths HL	DO Martin

T&W	Surname	Forename	Sex	Age	s/m/w	POB	Occup	Con date	Offence/sentence	Officer
1261	MULHOLLAND	Alice	F	18	S	Newcastle	Hawker	1873/04/17	Theft bed linen, 3 c/mths HL	DO S.Fawcett
1187	MULLEN	Bridget	F	17	S	Newcastle	Fact'y Hnd	1873/04/14	Theft shawl, 14 days HL	PC 21 M Lowtham
1087	MULLEN	John	M	18	S	Newcastle	Labourer	1872/10/07	Theft watch,4 c/mth HL	S.Fawcett
1216	MURRAY	Catherine	F	23	M	Glasgow	None	1873/05/01	Theft shawl, 1 c/mth HL	PC 19 Ferguson
1203	NAUGHTON	Patrick	M	29	S	Ireland	Boilermkr	1873/04/25	Theft watch, 1 c/mth HL	PC 35 J.Little
1221	O'NEIL	Patrick	M	19	S	Newcastle	Shoeblack	1871/12/12	Housebreaking,18 c/mths HL	Sgt. G.Anderson
1154	O'REGAN	John	M	18	S	Berwick	Labourer	1873/03/24	Theft beer, 14 days HL	Sgt.R.Anderson
1109	PARK	John	M	19	S	Scotland	Soldier RA	1873/01/27	Theft violin, 1 c/mth HL	PC 14 Smith
1276	PATTERSON	Mary	F	25	M	Newcastle	None	1873/06/24	Theft poultry, 6 wks HL	PC Webster
1175	PEARSON	Thomas	M	31	S	Humshaugh	R'way G'rd	1873/01/01	Theft ale, 4 c/mths HL	Insp Caig. NER
1200	RAMSHAW	Robert	M	35	S	Liverpool	Cartman	1873/02/24	Theft hams, 15 c/mths HL	PC J.K.Archbold
1173	RAY	George	M	30	M	Scotland	R'way G'rd	1873/01/01	Theft ale, 4 c/mths HL	Insp Craig NER
1183	REDHEAD	William	M	22	S	Newcastle	Cartman	1873/03/10	Theft coal, 2 c/mths HL	DO Martin
1135	REED	John	M	15	S	Gateshead	Glassmkr	1873/02/24	Theft money, 14 days HL, 5 yrs	PC J.McFadden
1227	RICHARDS	John	M	26	S	Plymouth	Hatter	1873/03/20	Theft money p, 3 c/mths HL	PC 14 J.Smith
1205	RICHLEY	James	M	30	M	Preston	W/hs/man	1873/04/29	Theft trivets, 7 days HL	PC S.Fawcett
1091	RIMINGTON	Richard	M	15	S	Newcastle	None	1873/01/17	Theft pipe, 14 days HL, 3 yrs	Sgt. R.Anderson
1102	RITCHIE	Barbara	F	35	M	Newcastle	None	1873/03/31	Theft coats, 7 days HL	Insp. Young
1167	ROBB	George	M	19	S	Scotland	Joiner	1872/10/29	Theft money p, 6 c/mth HL	Insp.Moss
1199	ROBINSON	Phillis or Mary	F	34	S	Alnwick	Prostitute	1873/04/24	Theft money p, 1 c/mth HL	Sgt..R.Anderson
1155	ROBSON	Isaac	M	16	S	Percy Main	Labourer	1873/03/24	Theft beer, 14 days HL	PC 10 Smith
1292	ROBSON	Joshua (junior)	M	19	S	Newcastle	Joiner	1873/02/24	Theft money, 6 c/mths HL	Sgt. Scott
1290	ROBSON	Joseph	M	23	S	Newcastle	Mason	1873/02/24	Theft iron, 6 c/mths HL	DO Martin
1136	ROMAN	John	M	64	M	Germany	Tailor	1873/02/24	Theft clothes, 14 days HL	PC J.Potts
1162	ROSS	Mary Ann	F	34	W	Edinburgh	Prostitute	1872/10/25	Theft money p, 6 c/mths HL	PC 28 T.Mowett
1284	ROURKE	Edward	M	17	S	Bedlington	Labourer	1873/06/13	Theft jacket, 2 c/mths HL	DO M.Thorburn

T&W	Surname	Forename	Sex	Age	s/m/w	POB	Occup	Con date	Offence/sentence	Officer
1084	RULE	Elizabeth	F	53	W	Edinburgh	Charw'n	1872/12/30	Theft shirt, 1 c/mth HL	PC 22 A.Guntrys
1170	RYAN	Dennis	M	20	S	Hartlepool	Puddler	1873/01/30	Theft money p, 3 c/mths HL	PC 27 W.Scott
1268	RYAN	Thomas	M	30	M	Belfast	Labourer	1873/01/23	Theft clothes, 6 c/mths HL	Sgt. R.Anderson
1115	SALMON	William	M	18	S	Dumfries	Puddler	1872/08/29	Theft clothes, 6 c/mth HL	DO S.Fawcett
1267	SCOTT	John	M	18	S	Sunderland	Labourer	1873/06/30	Theft iron bolt, 14 days HL	Sgt. James
1214	SCOTT	John	M	29	M	Newcastle	Labourer	1872/11/29	Theft lead 6 c/mths HL	Sgt. R.Anderson
1281	SCULLION	James	M	13	S	Newcastle	Labourer	1873/07/14	Theft clothes, 14 day HL, 3yrs	Sgt R.Anderson
1158	SHERVIN	Mary	F	21	S	Alnwick	Prostitute	1873/03/20	Theft money p, 1 c/mth HL	PC 5 McFaydon
1117	SHEVLIN	Edward	M	32	M	Ireland	Labourer	1872/09/03	Theft coat, 6 c/mths HL	DO Martin
1291	SHIELD	John	M	17	S	Newcastle	Labourer	1873/02/24	Theft money p, 6 c/mths HL	PC A.Stokoe
1224	SMITH	Mary	F	25	M	Belford	Hawker	1873/03/20	Theft money, 3 c/mths HL	PC 14 Smith
1149	SMITH	William	M	25	S	Sheffield	Printer	1873/02/10	Theft scales etc, 2 c/mths HL	PC 20 J.Relfe
1140	SMITH	Thomas	M	32	W	N Yk,USA	Shoem'ker	1873/01/01	Conspiracy, 3 c/mths HL	PC 27 J.Forster
1105	SMITH	Mary	F	50	M	Ireland	Charw'n	1873/02/04	Theft glass, 7 days HL	PC 30 M.Cockburn
1275	SMITH	Isabella	F	60	W	Elsdon	Charw'n	1873/06/24	Theft poultry, 6 weeks HL	DO S.Fawcett
1283	SNOWDON	Thomas	M	16	S	Newcastle	Clerk	1873/04/13	Theft cheque, 4 c/mths HL	DO G.Anderson
1168	SNOWDON	Joseph	M	18	S	Newcastle	Boatman	1872/10/29	Theft watch p, 6 c/mths HL	DO Martin
1165	STAFFORD	John	M	29	M	Newcastle	Striker	1873/03/24	Theft ham, 1 c/mth HL	PC 16 J.Archbold
1113	STEPHENSON	Henry Leonard	M	12	S	Cstle Eden	None	1873/01/01	Housebreaking, 2 c/mths HL	DO G.Anderson
1177	STEWART	Agnes	F	28	M	Edinburgh	Hawker	1872/10/31	Theft money p, 6 c/mths HL	Insp Martin
1279	STOREY	John	M	32	S	Newcastle	Labourer	1873/07/07	Theft wood, 1 c/mth HL	PC H.Beattie
1156	SUTHERLAND	Minnie	F	19	S	Sth. Shlds	Prostitute	1873/03/17	Theft clothes, 1 c/mth HL	PC 11 R.Moffatt
1108	SWEET	Samuel	M	24	M	Newcastle	Plumber	1872/12/26	Theft lead, 2 c/mths HL	DO Martin
1303	TAGG	John	M	21	S	Newcastle	Labourer	1873/05/30	Theft money p, 3 c/mth HL	PC M.Lowtham
1285	TAYLOR	John	M	26	M	Newcastle	Bricklyr	1873/07/15	Theft trowel, 1 c/mth HL	Sgt J.Martin
1188	TAYLOR	Michael	M	27	S	Newcastle	Slater	1873/02/10	Theft clothes, 3 c/mths HL	PC D.Tillie

T&W	Surname	Forename	Sex	Age	s/m/w	POB	Occup	Con date	Offence/sentence	Officer
1255	TAYLOR	Margaret	F	55	M	Berwick	Charw'n	1873/06/12	Theft coat, 1 c/mth HL	Sgt R.Anderson
1269	THOMAS	John	M	20	S	Newcastle	Soldier	1873/01/23	Theft slippers, 6 c/mths HL	PC T.Charlton
1151	THOMPSON	John	M	23	M	Gateshead	Platelyr	1873/03/21	Theft coal, 14 days HL	DO Hetherington
1254	THORLEY	Richard	M	29	S	Seghill	Miner	1873/03/14	Theft money p. 3 c/mths HL	PC 29 Grey
1166	TWEEDY	Thomas	M	20	S	Newcastle	Labourer	1872/12/26	Theft money p. 4 c/mths HL	PC 19 Ferguson
1129	WARDMAN	Thomas	M	20	S	Newcastle	Felter	1872/11/14	Theft money p. 4 c/mths HL	Sgt. J.Armstrong
1211	WATSON	Rosanna	F	13	S	Durham	None	1873/05/02	Theft iron, 7 days HL	PC 25 T.Lowrey
1138	WATSON	Thomas	M	40	M	Newcastle	Shoem'ker	1873/01/30	Theft boots, 2 c/mths HL	PC 20 J.Relfe
1163	WATSON	Mary Ann	F	42	M	Newcastle	None	1873/01/27	Theft money p. 3 c/mths HL	Sgt R.Anderson
1127	WIGGINS	Mary Ann	F	26	M	Newcastle	Prostitute	1873/02/10	Theft money p. 1 c/mth HL	PC 34 T.Hunter
1180	WIGHT	Richard/Robert	M	35	M	Glasgow	Dealer	1873/11/08	Theft pony, 6 c/mths HL	PC G.Dagg
1287	WILSON	James	M	23	S	Glasgow	Labourer	1873/04/17	Theft money p. 4 c/mths HL	PC 19 Ferguson
1202	WITHERS	Richard	M	26	M	N.America	Engineer	1873/03/24	Theft money p. 2 c/mths HL	PC M.Thorburn
1145	WOOD	Ann	F	30	M	Craml'gton	Prostitute	1873/02/06	Theft money p. 2 c/mths HL	PC 14 J.Smith
1209	WOODMAN	Ellen	F	11	S	Durham	None	1873/05/02	Theft iron, 7 days HL	PC 25 T.Lowrey
1088	WRIGHT	George	M	22	S	Newcastle	Striker	1873/10/08	Theft boots, 4 c/mth HL	DO M.Thorburn
1256	YATES	Ezekiel	M	35	M	Penrith	Grocer	1873/01/17	Theft tobacco, 6 c/mths HL	DO G.Anderson

Appendix 2: Accomplices

This is a schedule of the groups of accomplices or gangs identified during the research into this collection. The background stories for some of these gangs appear in the main text and may be found using the index.

The four-figure number before a name is the Tyne & Wear Archive number within Access No. PR/NC/6/1 as listed in Appendix No.1.

'(not listed)' means that the accomplice does not appear in the collection.

1082 Sarah Cassidy and 1083 Mary Ann Irving.

1111 Robert Johnson and 1112 Thomas Barclay.

1113 Henry Leonard Stephenson and 1172 Richard Clement Fisher.

1114 Robert Bolam, 1115 William Salmon and 1116 Thomas Garraty.

1121 Thomas Clementson and 1124 Joseph Calder.

1130 George Lamb, 1190 John Duffy and 1191 Peter Duffy.

1145 Ann Wood with John Penty and George Scott (neither listed).

1147 Margaret Middleton and 1156 Minnie Sutherland.

1154 John O'Regan and 1155 Isaac Robson.

1161 Mary Erskine Christie Thomas Christie and Michael Moan (neither listed).

1169 Barnard Connolly, 1170 Dennis Ryan and George Henderson (not listed).

1171 Richard Bradshaw and 1177 Agnes Stewart.

1173 George Ray 1174, Robert Hardy and 1175 Thomas Pearson.

1182 William Hope and 1183 William Redhead.

1194 Ann Kirk and James Newton (not listed).

1208 Mary Catherine Docherty, 1209 Ellen Woodman, 1210 Mary Hinnigan and 1211 Rosanna Watson.

1213 Mary Johnson and 1232 William Gordon.

1221 Patrick O'Neil, Francis McIntyre and Robert O'Hara (neither listed).

1224 Mary Smith and 1227 John Richards.

1230 Jane Carlisle, 1260 Catherine Kelly, 1261 Alice Mulholland and Margaret McIntyre (not listed).

1235 Joseph Jobey, 1236 Stephen Hunter and 1237 John Curry.

1242 Sabina Forbes and 1243 Margaret McCann.

1244 Catherine Cain and 1245 Maria Graham.

1251 James Loxley and 1252 Robert Cruddace.

1275 Isabella Smith and 1276 Mary Patterson.

1277 John Allan and 1278 Thomas Dixon.

1281 James Scullion and 1282 Henry Miller.

1284 Edward Rourke with Martin Wallace and Patrick Garaty (neither listed).

1287 James Wilson and William Douglas (not listed).

1293 Felix Mallon and Francis Wynn (not listed).

Partners in crime.
James Loxley and Robert
Cruddace (see page 120).

Reference and reading list

General

Newcastle Town, R.J.Charleton 1880, (reissued 1950 as *Charleton's History of Newcastle upon Tyne*, Harold Hill, Newcastle upon Tyne).

Newcastle upon Tyne, Its Growth and Achievement, Sydney Middlebrook (Newcastle Journal 1950).

Newcastle City Police (Newcastle Watch Committee 1969, prepared by the late Chief Superintendent W.J. Smith, Northumbria Police).

A History of English Prison Administration 1750-1877, Sean McConville (Routledge & Keegan Paul 1981).

Victorian prison Lives, English Prison Biography 1830-1914, Philip Priestly (Methuen 1985).

Constable, A History of the Northumbria Police, (written and published by Frederick C. Moffatt, 1993).

The Annual Reports of the Inspectors of Prisons, Scotland & Northern District 1836-1877 (Public Records).

Tyne and Wear Archive Service

Minutes of the Newcastle Watch Committee 1868-1874.

Newcastle gaol, Collection of Prison Forms and Photographs 1871-1873.

Newcastle Quarter Sessions Registers 1871-1874.

Local Studies, City Library, Newcastle upon Tyne

Tyneside Newspapers Collection.

Minutes of the proceedings of the Newcastle upon Tyne Town Council, annual volumes from 1836.

Report of the Committee Appointed to Examine Into Juvenile Crime in Newcastle and Gateshead 1852.

Newcastle as it is, Reviewed by its Moral Aspects, etc., Newcastle Temperance Society 1854.

The Devil's mudbath or the Unholy Slave Traffic in Newcastle upon Tyne, Newcastle Temperance Society 1883.

Census Returns 1871 & 1881, Statistical Analysis.

Report of the Medical Officer of Health on the Sanitary Condition of Newcastle upon Tyne for the Year 1874. (Henry E. Armstrong M.R.C.S., 1875).

Index of persons and places

Tyne & Wear Archives Service is the record office for the cities and metropolitan districts of Newcastle upon Tyne, Sunderland, Gateshead, South Tyneside and North Tyneside. It preserves documents relating to the area from the 12th to the 21st century, and the service is free for everyone to use.

Visit the Archives at
Blandford House, Blandford Square, Newcastle upon Tyne NE1 4JA

Or contact us in writing, by emailing twas@gateshead.gov.uk, or by telephoning 0191 2772248.

Find out more about the archives service at www.tyneandweararchives.co.uk